OECD
Economic Surveys

Mexico

2009

OECD

ORGANISATION FOR ECONOMIC CO-OPERATION AND DEVELOPMENT

The OECD is a unique forum where the governments of 30 democracies work together to address the economic, social and environmental challenges of globalisation. The OECD is also at the forefront of efforts to understand and to help governments respond to new developments and concerns, such as corporate governance, the information economy and the challenges of an ageing population. The Organisation provides a setting where governments can compare policy experiences, seek answers to common problems, identify good practice and work to co-ordinate domestic and international policies.

The OECD member countries are: Australia, Austria, Belgium, Canada, the Czech Republic, Denmark, Finland, France, Germany, Greece, Hungary, Iceland, Ireland, Italy, Japan, Korea, Luxembourg, Mexico, the Netherlands, New Zealand, Norway, Poland, Portugal, the Slovak Republic, Spain, Sweden, Switzerland, Turkey, the United Kingdom and the United States. The Commission of the European Communities takes part in the work of the OECD.

OECD Publishing disseminates widely the results of the Organisation's statistics gathering and research on economic, social and environmental issues, as well as the conventions, guidelines and standards agreed by its members.

Also available in French

Table of contents

Boxes

Tables

This Survey is published on the responsibility of the Economic and Development Review Committee of the OECD, which is charged with the examination of the economic situation of member countries.

The economic situation and policies of Mexico were reviewed by the Committee on 10 June 2009. The draft report was then revised in the light of the discussions and given final approval as the agreed report of the whole Committee on 23 June 2009.

The Secretariat's draft report was prepared for the Committee by Piritta Sorsa, Cyrille Schwellnus, Tonje Lauritzen, David Haugh and Agustin Redonda with statistical assistance from Roselyne Jamin, under the supervision of Patrick Lenain.

The previous Survey of Mexico was issued in September 2007.

This book has...

StatLinks

A service that delivers Excel® files from the printed page!

Look for the *StatLinks* at the bottom right-hand corner of the tables or graphs in this book. To download the matching Excel® spreadsheet, just type the link into your Internet browser, starting with the ***http://dx.doi.org*** prefix.
If you're reading the PDF e-book edition, and your PC is connected to the Internet, simply click on the link. You'll find *StatLinks* appearing in more OECD books.

BASIC STATISTICS OF MEXICO 2008

THE LAND

Area (sq. km)	1 964 375	Inhabitants in major metropolitan areas (millions), 2005	
Agriculture area (sq km) (1990)	394 000	Mexico City	19.3
		Guadalajara	4.2
		Monterrey	3.7

THE PEOPLE

Population (thousands)	106 683	Employment[1] (thousands)	43 517
Inhabitants per sq km	54.3		
Annual population growth (1990-2008)	1.3		

PRODUCTION

Structure of production		GDP (US$ billion)	1 085.3
(per cent of total, 2003 prices)		GDP per capita (US$, current prices	
Agriculture	3.6	and current PPPs)	14 431
Industry	30.3	Gross fixed capital formation	
of which: Manufacturing	17.6	(per cent of GDP, 2003 prices)	23.0
Services	63.3		

THE GOVERNMENT

			Senate	Chamber of Deputies
Public sector indicators (per cent of GDP)		Composition of Parliament (December)		
Public sector expenditure	26.9	PAN	52	206
Public sector total revenue	25.4	PRI	33	106
Oil-related revenue	10.8	PRD	26	127
		Other	17	61
Gross public debt (December)	39.3	Total	128	500

FOREIGN TRADE

Exports of merchandise (per cent of GDP)	28.3	Imports of merchandise (per cent of GDP)	30.5
Main exports (per cent of total)		Main imports (per cent of total)	
Manufactures	79.9	Intermediate goods	71.8
Petroleum products	17.4	Capital goods	12.7
Agriculture	2.7	Consumer goods	15.5

THE CURRENCY

Monetary unit: Peso	Currency units per US$, average of daily figures:	
	Year 2008	11.1352
	May 2009	13.1876

1. People economically active according to results of the Quarterly National Employment Survey.

Executive summary

Despite improved fundamentals, Mexico has not escaped the world economic recession. *The global manufacturing downturn and the collapse of trade, notably with the United States, have depressed the real sector. Reduced availability of credit has started to bear on activity, although the financial sector has so far weathered the global crisis. Low oil prices are putting pressure on budget revenue, despite a welcome hedging this year. The change of sentiment of international investors towards emerging-market borrowers has led to reduced net capital inflows and a large depreciation of the currency. The outbreak of influenza is likely to also contribute to the downturn. Thus, growth is set to be negative this year and recover only gradually in 2010. The authorities have responded with liquidity measures, lower interest rates, foreign currency interventions and a fiscal stimulus. But there might be room for more policy action.*

There is no space for further discretionary fiscal stimulus, *but automatic stabilizers should be allowed to operate freely until the recovery is well entrenched. Lower revenues could be partly compensated by drawing down the oil stabilization fund. To meet external financing requirements, the government has secured new financial resources from capital markets, multilateral lenders and the US Federal Reserve. Going forward, Mexico should seek to strengthen the counter-cyclical characteristics of the budget framework by adopting a fiscal rule adjusted for the cycle and smooth the injection of oil wealth into the economy. As oil extraction is likely to decline gradually over the next two decades, reforms are needed to reduce dependence on oil revenue.*

Health insurance coverage is incomplete and uneven across social groups, *which contributes to lower life expectancy and reduces the efficiency of health spending. Recent health reforms have been effective in providing basic health care to some of the poorest groups, but achieving universal coverage by 2011 will remain challenging. In addition, the existence of separate, vertically integrated insurance networks increases administrative costs. Further reforms are also needed to reduce the fragmentation of the health system.*

The coverage of lower secondary education is inadequate as only two-thirds of the relevant age group attends schools. *Furthermore, poor PISA scores reflect low teaching quality, a consequence of non-transparent teacher selection processes until recently and limited school autonomy. Accountability to the government and parents is also low. The Alianza reform makes a promising step in the direction of addressing these problems and should be fully implemented.*

Structural reforms in key areas are needed to boost long-term growth, *which has been weaker than in many other emerging economies. The recent significant reductions in import tariffs should help the economy take fuller advantage of trade and investment integration, which could be a relative strength for Mexico given its geographic location. In addition to education and health, further measures are needed to enhance product-market competition, especially in network industries, promote the rule of law and build much-needed transportation infrastructure. The investment regime is too restrictive in some sectors (such as telecommunication and energy) and should be liberalised. Persisting with structural reforms despite the recession would support both short-term recovery and longer-term growth.*

ISBN 978-92-64-05441-7
OECD Economic Surveys: Mexico
© OECD 2009

Assessment and recommendations

Despite improved macroeconomic fundamentals,
Mexico is being hit hard by the financial crisis
and world economic downturn

Mexico is affected severely by the global recession, like many other OECD countries, with negative economic, budgetary and social consequences. Although the banking sector has so far weathered the financial crisis rather well, manufacturing industries are being severely affected by the downturn of global demand, particularly in high-value added industries. Shipments of goods to US markets have plummeted at a fast pace, following a global readjustment of industrial inventories and leading to a sharp contraction of industrial production. Like other emerging markets, Mexico has suffered from reduced net capital inflows, as investments returned to safer havens, contributing to a decline in equity prices, rising interest rate spreads and a large depreciation of the peso. In addition, several country-specific shocks have had adverse consequences, such as the outbreak of influenza A H1N1. Also, the budget has been put under pressure by the sharp decline in energy prices, as oil exports provide a large share of tax revenues, although temporary relief comes from a price hedge and weaker peso. The rise in uncertainty has depressed business and consumer confidence to record lows, which, coupled with tightening credit conditions at home and abroad, is bearing on consumption and investment. Despite the slowdown in activity and declining commodity prices, inflation has remained persistently high as prices of tradables and food are adjusting with a lag.

In this environment, it is likely that growth will be sharply negative in 2009 with only a moderate recovery in 2010. The sharp and broad-based drop in activity is set to increase unemployment, which is projected to reach levels last seen during the financial crisis of 1994-1995. As pressures from high commodity prices wear off and the output gap widens, inflation is likely to recede and reach its target by the end of 2010. With monetary and fiscal stimulus taking hold and world activity picking up, demand should stabilize with quarterly growth rates becoming positive towards end 2009 and reaching about 4% in annualised terms by end 2010. Risks to the outlook remain on the downside, driven by continued uncertainties with world financial markets and growth. Risks can also arise from foreign financing needs, if conditions for emerging markets worsen further.

Macroeconomic stability and increased policy
credibility has helped to deflect severe
financial stress

Since the Tequila crisis in 1994-95, which caused a dramatic output contraction, much progress has been made in improving macroeconomic policies, reducing economic imbalances and restoring policy credibility. The inflation-targeting framework has been successful in better anchoring price expectations. The fiscal rule has been instrumental in achieving balanced federal budgets and reducing public indebtedness. The development of domestic bond markets and a pro-active debt management strategy have increased maturities and substituted foreign for domestic debt, thereby reducing exposure to currency and rollover risks. The low current account deficits, in turn, have lowered foreign financing needs. The build-up of foreign reserves, facilitated by the rise in oil prices, the swap with the US Federal Reserve and the IMF's Flexible Credit Line, provided another cushion to face economic shocks. Reflecting this better policy environment, Mexico has avoided the type of full-blown financial stress currently experienced by some other emerging markets, although it could not totally protect the real sector from the global downturn.

Monetary policy has become more supportive,
but interest rates might be lowered further

Although there was a cycle of global monetary easing that, in general, started in the third quarter for industrialized economies and in the fourth quarter for some emerging markets, Mexico's central bank kept its policy rates unchanged so as to contain inflation expectations at a time when inflation was increasing. Monetary policy loosening took place later than in other OECD countries, reflecting risks of additional capital outflows and further exchange rate pressure. With price pressures showing signs of levelling off in early 2009 and activity on a clear downward trend, policy rates were lowered in several rapid steps. *The deterioration of economic activity in Mexico might provide room for a further lowering of policy rates, so as to sustain demand and improve financial conditions, while keeping an eye on the evolution of actual and expected inflation.* Quantitative estimates suggest that exchange-rate pass through has become more limited, reflecting strengthened policy credibility and better anchored inflation expectations, so it will be important to preserve this hard-won credibility. In an environment of tight credit supply and weak market prospects, lower interest rates may not have a large direct effect on consumption and investment, but it could have some beneficial effects on confidence.

The authorities should remain vigilant
in monitoring overall financial stability,
including corporate balance sheets

The financial sector looked relatively sound at the onset of the crisis and its limited exposure to foreign assets and liabilities reduced vulnerability to shocks. Conservative lending policies helped contain credit demand and avoided housing bubbles. The sector remains well capitalised and profitable, which partly reflects strict prudential regulations that limited banks' asset exposure to currency risk and risky products. High net interest margins and operating costs also provide some cushion for absorbing losses. However, the financial indicators tend to be backward looking and can change rapidly as the economy worsens. The weakening economy and declining asset prices may lead to second-round effects on Mexican banks with a feedback to the real economy. Both consumers and enterprises may find it difficult to service their debts, thus affecting the quality of bank portfolios. Vulnerabilities might also arise from the enterprise sector, which relies on foreign sources for close to half of its credit needs, if maturing foreign debt cannot be rolled over. *These risks should be monitored closely by the authorities.*

A welcome fiscal stimulus package in 2009

Fiscal policy has been prudently guided by a framework aiming at balanced budgets and saving part of oil revenues in a stabilization fund. The framework has contributed to securing long-term sustainability and improved policy credibility. The fiscal stimulus measures in the 2009 budget and the January 2009 package to stimulate demand, which account for 1.6% of GDP, are broadly welcome. In particular, the increase in infrastructure spending, subsidies to employment and increased social transfers with sunset clauses should smooth the downturn. However, the fiscal package contained provision to freeze nominal energy prices, which is a socially-regressive form of support and an inefficient type of economic stimulus. *Shifting more of the stimulus to support employment and incomes would enhance its impact on demand and protect workers from falling into poverty.*

Fiscal policy should remain supportive in 2010

Budget revenues are projected to fall in 2010, reflecting the depressing effect of low world energy prices on oil revenue and the negative influence of the downswing on non-oil tax revenue. While oil revenue has been protected in 2009 by a hedge on oil export prices, this advantage will disappear in 2010. Thus, the OECD's *Economic Outlook* projects that the government deficit (in terms of net lending or public sector net borrowing requirement) will increase from some 3-4% of GDP in 2009 to about 5% of GDP in 2010, assuming no corrective measures to cut expenditure or raise taxes. Mexico would be able to cover this level of borrowing, including by drawing down oil stabilization funds that were accumulated during the past period of high energy prices. To help meet external financing requirements, the government has secured large sources of foreign lending from the capital market, multilateral agencies and the US Federal Reserve. *The stance of fiscal policy should not turn restrictive in 2010, as ongoing support to domestic demand will remain necessary to combat the economic downturn; thus the deficit should be allowed to increase by the amount of automatic stabilizers, considering the use of the stabilization funds for the financing of this deficit while at the same time not imperilling long-term fiscal sustainability.* The preliminary budgetary projections for 2010 submitted by the government go in this direction: the expected fall in oil-related revenues is financed by drawing down oil stabilization funds.

Mexico faces the challenge of managing oil revenue

Like other large oil-exporting countries, Mexico faces the challenge of managing the macroeconomic impact of oil revenue. While such revenue provides useful resources to the economy, its management raises a number of difficult issues. Oil revenue tends to be highly volatile and the budget risks channelling this volatility to the non-oil parts of the economy; indeed, in Mexico, public consumption and GDP are highly volatile by OECD standards. In addition, because oil price fluctuations tend to be synchronized with the world economic cycle, the budget has a tendency for pro-cyclicality, with more spending in good times and spending cuts during downturns. This is reinforced in Mexico by the balanced-budget rule, which requires matching the swings in revenues by parallel swings in spending.

Thus, the fiscal framework should be adjusted to better shield public expenditure from the high volatility of oil revenue. In some countries, this is achieved by transferring the bulk of oil wealth to future generations, thus minimizing the injection of oil revenue into domestic demand. In Mexico, however, it seems both efficient and fair that the current generation uses oil revenue to finance economic development, so as to raise present as well as future living standards. Hence, fiscal policy should seek to smooth the injection of oil revenue into the economy over the cycle and avoid abrupt changes in public spending. Mexico established several oil-stabilization funds for this purpose but accumulated savings were capped at relatively low levels, which made the funds less useful for the purpose of macroeconomic stabilization. The recent decision to raise the maximum size of the oil stabilization funds goes in the right direction, but *Mexico should consider eliminating this limit altogether. Also, like other oil-exporting countries, Mexico should seek to strengthen the counter cyclical framework of the budget, by adopting a new fiscal rule adjusted for the cycle.* This would lead to prudent fiscal management practices including *a)* smooth growth of public spending in line with economic growth, *b)* automatic savings of oil revenue above what is implied by the rule when the oil price is high and *c)* automatic spending of accumulated savings when oil revenue is low. This would improve the role played by fiscal policy in macroeconomic management, would phase in gradually the injection of oil wealth into the economy and would contribute to long-term sustainability. The appropriate level of the limit on the structural non-oil deficit would depend on various factors, many of which come with large uncertainties, such as level of oil extraction. *Given these uncertainties, the limit for the non-oil structural deficit should be reviewed regularly, so as to stabilize the net financial position of the public sector:* increases in net financial assets would suggest that there is space for running a higher non-oil structural deficit, while increases in net financial liabilities would call for tightening the non-oil structural deficit target.

Public finances should be prepared for the long term decline of oil

---

Declining oil production will squeeze the contributions made by PEMEX to the budget over the next two decades, putting pressure on social spending and infrastructure development. It is therefore essential to prepare the public finances for this decline. The recent reforms to improve governance of Pemex are welcome, but more needs to be done. The policy of keeping gasoline prices constant in real terms – which at times implies lower prices than in the United States –, and subsidies on LP gas and electricity for household use, are inefficient and unfair. *Instead, gasoline prices should move in line with international reference prices, an energy excise tax should be introduced, and subsidies on other energy products should be removed.* Keeping gasoline and energy prices at present low levels comes with few benefits: empirical research shows that the subsidy is mainly captured by well-off social groups and tends therefore to be regressive; it also leads to a distortion in the allocation of resources, reducing interest for alternative and sustainable sources of energy; finally it encourages the burning of hydrocarbons, with detrimental effects on greenhouse gas emissions and global climate change. While helping low-income groups with the price of energy might be a legitimate social goal, this can be achieved in better ways, for instance with means-tested income support schemes or subsidies to cooking gas in poor areas. It is also essential to boost the non-oil tax base. About 30-40% of budget revenues depend on oil, while non-oil taxes are only about 10% of GDP, which is low compared to peers or the social needs of Mexico. While recent tax reforms are welcome, *more needs to be done to broaden the tax base.* Further reform that tackles in particular exemptions in both direct and indirect taxes is needed in line with recommendations in the 2007 *Survey*. Finally, more needs to be done to raise the efficiency of public spending in education and health, as discussed below.

Spending efficiency in health can be improved

Although public spending per capita on health has more than doubled in real terms since the 1995 financial crisis, it remains low by international standards. At the same time, Mexico's health indicators lag behind those of most OECD countries. Although population health indicators have improved over the past two decades, life expectancy at birth remains lower, child mortality higher and outcomes highly uneven across socioeconomic groups. While this partly reflects Mexico's lower per capita income, incomplete coverage and fragmentation in services provision contribute to poor outcomes. Further spending pressures will arise from the plan to achieve universal health insurance by 2011. While additional spending may help, improving health outcomes will result primarily from increasing the efficiency of spending. Although current reforms go into the right direction, better outcomes in some Latin American countries with similar per capita income and spending suggest that there is further scope for improving the efficiency of the health sector in Mexico.

The fragmentation of the health system should be reduced

The fragmentation of the health care system into several separate units that vertically integrate financing, insurance and provision functions contributes to inefficiencies, including by duplicating facilities and by increasing costs. The social security institutes cover salaried workers in the formal sector, while the "popular health insurance" scheme (*Seguro Popular*) covers part of the population working in the informal sector and non-salaried formal workers. There is no split between insurer and provider functions, which has reduced quality of services and led to cost inefficiencies because money does not flow to the highest-quality and most efficient providers. To reduce administrative costs in health systems with multiple insurers, other OECD countries have introduced centralized claims management systems. While the health reform of 2004 and current policies, including the sharing of new facilities between insurers, address some of these issues, there is further scope for improving the efficiency of spending. *A clear split between the functions of insurer and provider of care should be introduced throughout the system and any insurer should be allowed to contract with any provider. Administrative costs could be reduced by introducing a unified claims management system.*

Universal health coverage may require making
insurance mandatory

One third of the population, mostly in low-income groups, has no health insurance, which has contributed to poor health outcomes. The uninsured are less likely to receive appropriate preventive care and timely treatment when sick, which results in higher spending, often out-of-pocket, and worse outcomes. The government is aiming for universal coverage by 2011 by further expanding *Seguro Popular*, which has been successful in increasing coverage by about 25% of the population since 2004. However, coverage should be made mandatory to ensure nobody is inadvertently left uncovered and to contain adverse selection (the healthy may avoid paying premiums) that could undermine the finances of the programme. This is a key lesson from the experience of other OECD countries that have recently adopted universal health insurance. To achieve this, *the authorities should enter discussions about making health insurance mandatory and identifying resources to finance the likely increase in public spending in a sustainable way.*

Enrolment into secondary education should
be enhanced through an expansion
of conditional cash transfers to poor students

Mexico's relatively poor PISA scores and low secondary school enrolment are strongly related to socio-economic backgrounds. Less than 50% of children from households in the bottom decile of the income distribution attend secondary school, in contrast to more than 80% in the top decile. To improve coverage in secondary education, the government has recently introduced the *Jóvenes con Oportunidades* programme that gives cash grants conditional upon secondary school completion. *Expanding the scope of this programme can be a good way of increasing coverage and spending efficiency in education.*

Education outcomes would benefit from
implementing the Alianza quality-enhancing
programme and improving incentives in schools

Education outcomes in Mexico are also influenced by poor school and teaching quality. Until recently, the teacher selection process was not transparent, and the main teacher incentive scheme continues to put excessive weight on seniority, which lowers teaching quality. Schools have limited autonomy in budgeting, instruction and personnel and there is no national exit exam after secondary education that would make schools accountable to the government and parents. In other OECD countries greater autonomy and exit exams have been major factors in improving teaching quality. Existing evaluation programmes that focus on rote knowledge instead of analytical capabilities, and the undercapitalisation of the school system, are also likely to have contributed to poor PISA scores. Some of these issues are being addressed by recent reforms such as the quality school programme and the (voluntary) Alliance for quality education. This agreement between the government and the main teachers' union should be implemented country-wide. *In particular, the teacher selection process should be based on a nation-wide entry exam, as planned by the Alliance and implemented for the first time in 2008. Incentives for teachers should be more closely linked to teaching performance and existing evaluation schemes should be consolidated and focused on analytical capabilities instead of knowledge.*

Mexico's living standards are catching up only slowly

Though improving, the growth performance in Mexico over the past 20 years has been disappointing when compared to other emerging markets, reflecting mainly weak labour productivity growth, which was slightly negative over the period. A breakdown by industry shows that the poor performance was broad based – the weak relative performance of productivity applies to about 80% of total employment. Growth in Mexico has relied more on the accumulation of production factors, notably the utilisation of labour resources, than on rising productivity. By contrast, the better performing countries, such as Chile and Turkey exhibit an "intensive" growth path, with a greater reliance on high labour productivity growth rates. However, breaking down Mexico's performance into 5-year periods reveals a more encouraging story, as productivity growth has increased continuously from each 5-year period to the next. Although productivity and per capita GDP growth rates have increased, they remain too low to allow rapid convergence with the high-income OECD countries.

Mexico's slow catch up towards higher levels of incomes is mainly due to the lack of progress with some growth-friendly structural reforms. OECD regulatory impact indicators show that Mexico is in many key sectors close to, or equal to, the maximum (negative) regulatory impact, and that Mexican productivity would be higher with less strict product-market regulation. The largest negative impact is in the network industries (electricity, gas and water) where Mexico's product-market regulation is much stricter than in most other OECD countries.

Structural reforms should continue to boost productivity growth

The recent significant reductions in import tariffs should help the economy take fuller advantage of trade and investment integration, which could be a relative strength for Mexico given its geographic location. Reforms introduced in the past two years, including those to promote competition and transparency in the financial sector and, to a lesser extent in telecommunications, will also stimulate the dynamism of the economy. Despite this progress, further reforms are needed to boost overall and within-sector productivity. Relative weaknesses in education, infrastructure, financial development, the rule of law, trade integration and investment levels, especially in machinery and equipment, as well as a lack of competition arising from overly restrictive product market regulation and excessive state control come out in various studies as explaining why Mexico has not grown as fast as other countries. Science, technology and innovation policies can also be important over time as noted in the OECD *Review of Innovation Policy* in Mexico.

High priority should be given to structural reforms
with rapid payoffs

There are certain structural reforms that can both help countries exit from the financial crisis and provide longer-term growth benefits. Potentially rapid pay-offs can be obtained from *reforms in education and training, and from reducing entry barriers to business*. These can boost demand by improving employment prospects and growth by enhancing future productivity. *Increasing competition can bring gains to productivity over time, and recent efforts in this area should be continued without delay*. The road, rail, port and telecommunication networks remain weak compared to those in its emerging market peers. In this context, the rise in infrastructure spending in the 2009 budget is welcome. The decision to conduct a broad review of existing regulatory policies is an important step towards reducing a key structural barrier to faster growth. *There is scope for regulatory action to increase competition in the main network industries, electricity, gas, water, telecommunications and transport*. Greater competition would also help safeguard gains of competitiveness from the lower exchange rate by containing price pressures.

ISBN 978-92-64-05441-7
OECD Economic Surveys: Mexico
© OECD 2009

Chapter 1

Overcoming the financial crisis and the macroeconomic downturn

Despite improved fundamentals Mexico is being hit by the financial turmoil and world economic downturn. As in other emerging markets, there has been a reduction in net capital inflows, which contributed to a large depreciation of the peso in the last quarter of 2008 and in the first months of 2009, although since then the peso has stabilized at a lower level. Access to foreign capital has become more restricted and costly. With a relatively small and well regulated financial sector Mexico has been able to weather the initial shock. The global recession has, however, hit the real sector through the trade channel, reflecting the heavy dependence on the US market. Another shock is the collapse of oil prices, which is depressing fiscal revenues, though these prices have recovered with respect to the minimum levels observed at the end of 2008. Business and consumer confidence have fallen considerably. The outbreak of influenza is also likely to contribute to the downturn. Growth is set to drop substantially this year and start to recover slowly next year. The authorities have responded with liquidity measures, foreign currency interventions, lower interest rates, external borrowing and fiscal stimulus. There might be some room for more monetary easing, if the economy deteriorates further, while fiscal stimulus should be better targeted. The scope for further fiscal measures is limited by uncertainties of future oil revenues, higher cost of funding and the risk of inefficient spending. Although banks remain sound, the authorities should closely monitor bank portfolios, which may be adversely affected by the worsening economic outlook.

The macroeconomic outlook is worsening rapidly

The improved macroeconomic management since the Tequila crisis in 1994 has enhanced economic stability and increased Mexico's ability to weather shocks. The gradual implementation of an inflation targeting regime since 1999 has boosted monetary policy credibility and helped anchor inflation expectations. Inflation declined to low single digits in a few years. Macroeconomic stability was supported by broadly prudent fiscal policy and active debt management. Total and foreign currency gross public debt stood at 40% and 9% of GDP respectively at end 2008, which reduced vulnerabilities to external shocks. Confidence was boosted further by the accumulation of a foreign currency reserve buffer and strengthening of prudential supervision. This sound economic management was facilitated by strong growth, low real interest rates and booming international commodity prices, which helped to compensate for the high dependence of public finances on volatile oil revenues.

The intensification of the financial crisis, the global economic downturn and the decline in energy prices have put Mexico's macroeconomic policy mix to a new test. After reviewing recent developments, including the financial and real sector impact of the crisis on Mexico, and the outlook, Chapter 1 looks at the appropriateness of current macroeconomic policies and their mix in the context of a more volatile world economy. It discusses the evolution of the fiscal stance over the last cycle, and the role of fiscal policy in dealing with the turmoil in the short-run (counter cyclicality, fiscal policy effectiveness). In this context current fiscal rules and the fiscal challenges arising from the oil sector are important. The chapter also discusses monetary policy challenges against the backdrop of inflationary pressures, a depreciating currency and a slowing economy and touches upon financial sector issues.

Policymaking in Mexico continues to be complicated by the heavy dependence of the budget on the large oil sector. Over a third of budgetary income is related to the volatile oil sector, leading to high volatility in revenues in the current context of large swings in international commodity prices, and spending, especially with the balanced budget rule. The oil curse (or blessing) also affects competitiveness by its tendency to appreciate the real exchange rate (Dutch disease). Furthermore, as the oil sector in Mexico is publicly owned by constitution and is part of the regular budget, funds for its future development compete with other public resources. Some of these issues have been recently addressed by steps towards broadening the tax base and starting to reform the state oil company, Pemex, but many challenges remain. The fiscal management of oil revenues is discussed in more detail in Chapter 2. Chapter 3 looks at efficiency of social spending that has a role to play in reducing inequalities and sustaining growth.

Despite good macroeconomic management, lagging structural reforms have impeded progress in raising growth and reducing inequalities. Growth averaged 2.9% per annum over the past decade, leaving Mexico far behind its emerging market peers in raising living standards. Growth has also failed to reduce inequalities which over time can spark resistance to pro-growth policies. Even though the pace of reforms has picked up, they have still been insufficient to eliminate all the structural weaknesses that hold back productivity and potential growth. These relate in particular to education and health, competition and infrastructure, and are discussed in more detail in Chapter 4, building on past surveys.

A mild financial crisis but a severe downturn of output

Following a long expansion, growth started to cool from mid-2008 as the world outlook worsened in the wake of the deepening world financial crisis. The solid growth around potential since 2002, driven by consumption and investment started to fade in 2008. Private consumption was hit by declining real wages and lower remittances from emigrants in the United States, while investment demand has waned in response to the continuously worsening world outlook. Exports, which depend heavily on US markets, were adversely affected by the drop in US industrial production, declining oil prices and lower-than-expected oil output at home. In contrast, growth in public consumption and investment has been stronger, boosted by higher and non-oil revenues in the budget (Figure 1.1). The outlook deteriorated significantly as from September 2008 as the financial crisis deepened.

Figure 1.1. **Contribution to growth**[1]

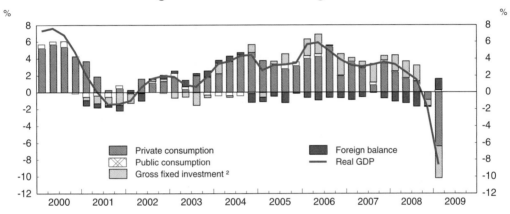

1. As a percentage of real GDP in same quarter of previous year.
2. Including stockbuilding.

Source: OECD, National Accounts.

StatLink http://dx.doi.org/10.1787/683062281310

Mexico was better prepared in 2008 than in past decades to face external shocks. Broadly sound fiscal and monetary policies in an inflation-targeting framework have reduced macroeconomic imbalances, and increased policy credibility. The low current account deficits, in turn, have reduced foreign financing needs. The development of domestic bond markets[1] and a pro-active debt management strategy have increased maturities and substituted foreign for domestic debt, thereby reducing public sector exposure to currency and rollover risks. The build-up of foreign reserves, facilitated by rising oil prices, provided another cushion to face financial turmoil, although the stock of accumulated reserves at about 7% of GDP at end-2008 remained relatively small compared to that of other emerging economies. Mexico's net liabilities to foreigners, at about 40% of GDP in 2007, were about average compared to other emerging markets (Figure 1.2) and vulnerabilities were low compared to past crisis episodes.[2]

The financial sector looked relatively sound at the onset of the crisis and its limited exposure to foreign assets or liabilities reduces vulnerability to shocks. An appropriately

Figure 1.2. **Mexico's net international investment position**

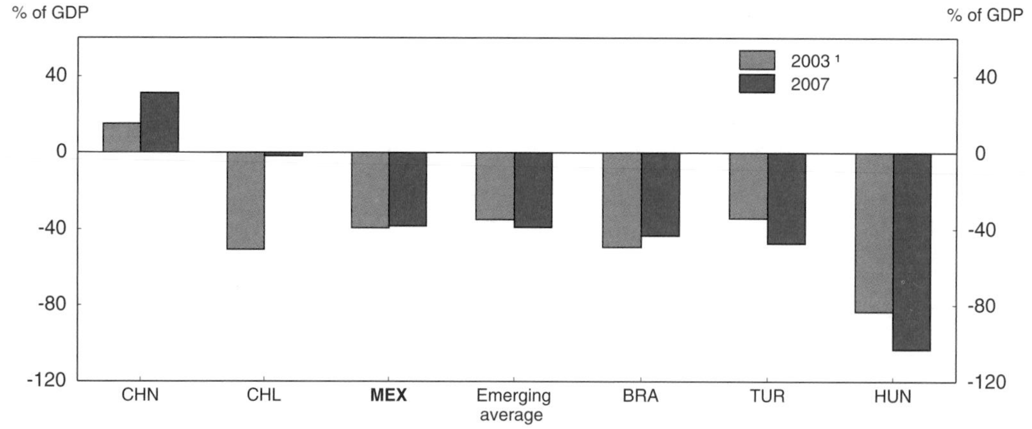

1. 2004 for China.
Source: IMF, International Financial Statistics.

StatLink http://dx.doi.org/10.1787/683066750727

restrictive monetary stance and conservative lending policies helped contain credit demand and avoid housing bubbles. Credit supply has been affected by high transaction costs in case of default and attractive investment opportunities in less risky government paper, Nevertheless, annual real credit growth has been over 20 per cent in recent years, albeit from a low base. The banking sector has been well capitalised and profitable with low overall exposure to risky assets or foreign liabilities (Table 1.1). This partly reflects the low starting point so the expansion took place with banks providing credit to customers with high credit-worthiness, limited competition that has sustained high profits with relatively low risk (Haber 2006), especially in the larger banks, and also strict prudential regulations that limited banks' asset exposure to currency risk and risky products. Stress tests by the central bank in early 2008 indicated an ability to withstand various shocks (Banxico 2008). The highest risks are with consumer credit, which has experienced its fastest growth in recent years.

Table 1.1. **Mexico: Selected financial soundness indicators**

End 2008

	Capital adequacy	NPL	ROA	Leverage assets/equity	Risk exposure RWA/ Assets
Mexico	16	2.1	2.9	9.8	64.2
Brazil	18.1	2.9	2.8	10.4	68.1
Chile	12.3	0.9	1.1	14.1	76.7
United States	12.8	1.7	0.6	9.7	78.6

Note: ROA = return on assets; NPL = non-performing loans; RWA = risk weighed assets.
Source: Banxico, IMF.

However, as in many other countries, important financial disturbances were observed and important risks remained, as reflected in the rise in Mexico's sovereign spreads since August 2008 and pressures on the peso at the end of 2008 and the first months of 2009:

● *The increased reliance on portfolio capital* in recent years makes Mexico vulnerable to capital outflows and changes in market sentiment. Mexico, like other emerging markets in Latin America, had attracted large portfolio inflows—foreign equity holdings rose from 8% to 15%

of GDP and non-residents have financed a steady 1% of GDP of domestic bonds since 2001. The inflows into domestic bond markets had intensified during 2008 up until September, attracted by the rise in the interest rate differential with the US and an appreciating peso.

● *Mexican enterprises relied on foreign sources for close to half of their credit needs*, which makes them vulnerable to currency risks and changes in lending conditions abroad. In previous years, high domestic real interest rates and expectations of an appreciating peso made foreign credit attractive.

● *Public sector revenues depend heavily on oil income.* About 30-40% of budgetary revenues are from oil. The current lower level of the oil price, if sustained, coupled with projected drops in production volumes, could lead to a substantial increase in the public sector financing requirement.

● *Dependence on the US economy is high.* As a small open economy with very strong links to the United States, Mexico is vulnerable to real sector effects of world financial turmoil. About 80% of its exports are destined to the United States, which makes developments in that market particularly important.

Impact of the financial crisis

The turmoil first hit Mexican capital markets as risk-aversion among foreign investors intensified in September 2008. The peso came under pressure as foreign portfolio investors pulled out from Mexican capital markets in the last quarter of 2008. The pressure on the currency was intensified by demand for dollars by a reduced number of large domestic enterprises to cover up their exposures on foreign exchange derivatives. The peso depreciated by about 30% against the dollar in a month. Interventions in the exchange market by the central bank and the announcement of a swap facility with the US Federal Reserve helped stabilise markets. The pressure on the stock market was further intensified by portfolio adjustments by domestic investment funds to meet their value at risk requirements. Equity prices fell and foreign bond spreads shot up as perceptions of risk changed. The search for short-term liquidity further disrupted domestic bond markets causing a large spike in long-term risk premia (Figure 1.3). The bond markets were

Figure 1.3. **Public sector interest rates**

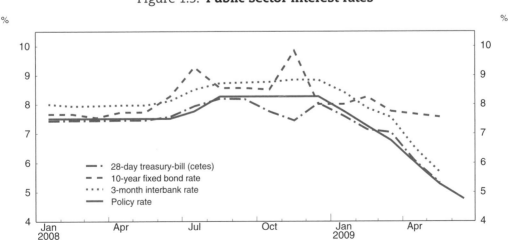

Source: Banco de México and INEGI.

StatLink ᵃᵐˢᵖ *http://dx.doi.org/10.1787/683108607821*

stabilised only after a number of temporary interventions by the government both at the short and long ends.[3]

The immediate financial impact of the intensification of the crisis on Mexico was around average among emerging markets. The rise in its CDS spread between August and December 2008 was close to the average, and the 20% drop in the stock market index was moderate compared to other emerging markets (Figure 1.4). On the other hand, the depreciation of the currency was among the largest among them reflecting in part the oil-related terms of trade shock and the drop in US demand, in addition to the financial one. Clearly, Mexico is one of the economies with the highest trade links with the US economy. Although most emerging markets have been affected by repricing of risk, those with good

Figure 1.4. **Changes in the stock market index and the exchange rate after the intensification of the crisis**

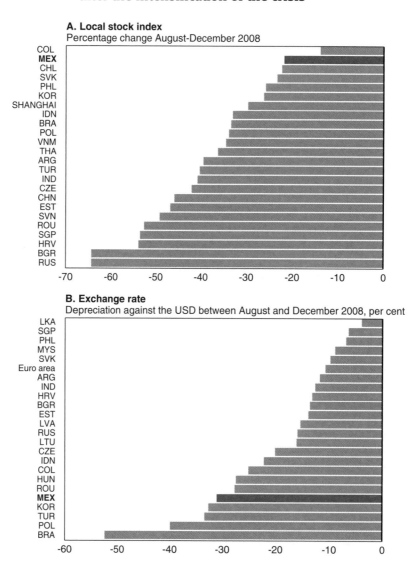

A. Local stock index
Percentage change August-December 2008

B. Exchange rate
Depreciation against the USD between August and December 2008, per cent

Source: Banco de México; Datastream.

StatLink http://dx.doi.org/10.1787/683245320316

macroeconomic fundamentals and moderate vulnerabilities, such as Mexico have fared better (Figure 1.5). Thus while improved policies did not spare Mexico from the financial crisis, they are likely to have mitigated its impact.

Figure 1.5. **Changes in emerging market spreads and fundamentals**

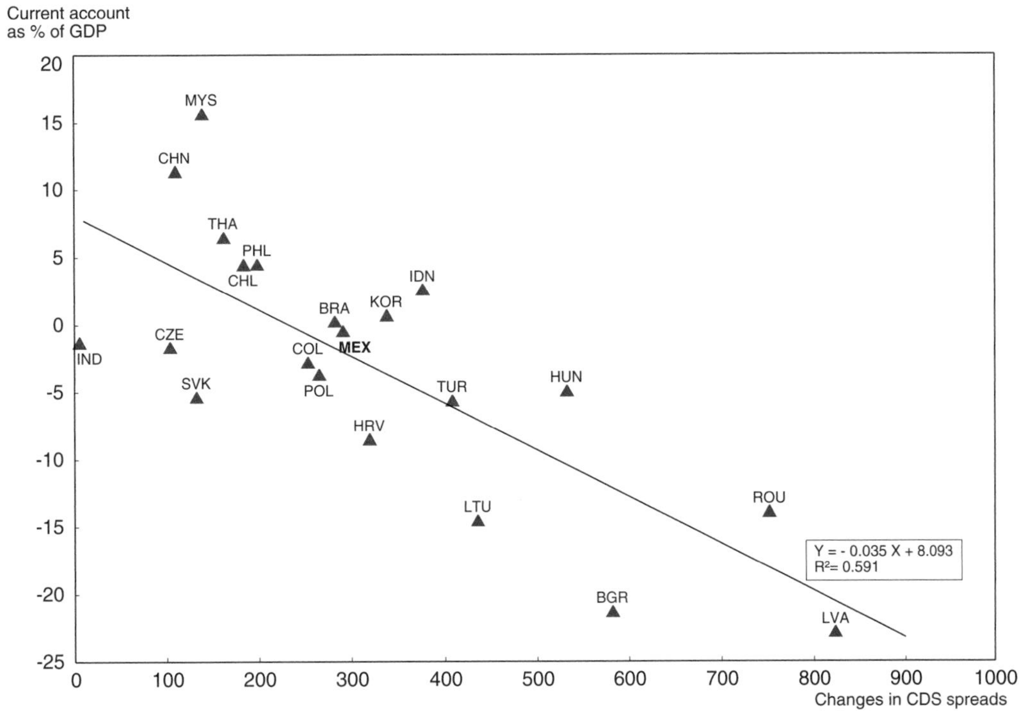

1. Between August 1 and mid-December 2008 in bp.
Source: Datastream.

StatLink ᔑᓯᒣ http://dx.doi.org/10.1787/683340148781

Subsequently, markets in Mexico as in many other emerging markets, have stabilized somewhat. The risk premia have trended downwards with respect to the maximum levels observed during the first quarter of 2009, the peso/dollar exchange rate has appreciated and its volatility has fallen significantly. The oil price has staged an important recovery. Towards mid-2009 there were also signs that Mexican enterprises had adjusted their financing needs, as evidenced by limited demand for dollar funds in auctions of resources from the swap with the Federal Reserve that was carried out by Banco de México.

Mexico is also being affected via the credit channel, although the impact is reduced by the low level of financial deepening. Risk aversion by foreign lenders has increased sovereign spreads (Figure 1.6) and reduced credit to Mexico. This affects mostly the enterprise sector, which is the main user of foreign loans. But as foreign enterprise credit was only about 5% of GDP[4] the economic impact may be limited. Some large enterprises have issued commercial paper abroad, which are more expensive and potentially harder to rollover in the current environment (Banxico 2009). Despite a foreign dominance in the domestic banking sector (80% of assets), strict prudential rules on open foreign positions have limited the use of foreign funding by banks.[5] However, domestic credit supply is being affected as both domestic and foreign banks have tightened credit in the context of a sharp slowdown in economic activity and higher uncertainty. Demand for credit in turn is

Figure 1.6. **Risk premiums**

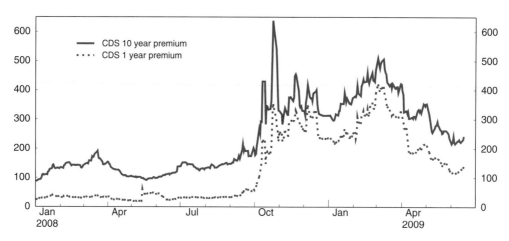

Source: Banco de México.

StatLink ⟨⟩ http://dx.doi.org/10.1787/683437387513

reduced by rising costs especially for households (Figure 1.7), lower wealth and uncertainty about the economic outlook (Figure 1.8). The decline in private credit growth has been significant from over 20% in annual terms until mid-2008 to less than 1% in April 2009, potentially restricting consumption and investment. Indeed, consumer credit is declining. However, with the credit/GDP ratio at only a fifth of GDP the economic impact of the credit crunch is reduced.

Figure 1.7. **Private sector interest rates**

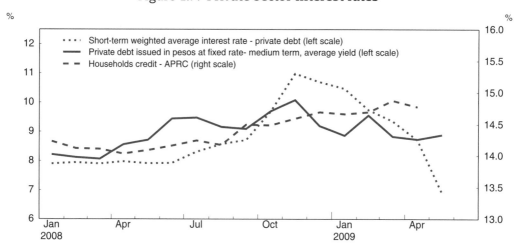

Source: Banco de México.

StatLink ⟨⟩ http://dx.doi.org/10.1787/683452468353

Mexican banks were well prepared to face the turmoil. The quality of bank supervision in Mexico has been generally considered good in international surveys and stress tests (IMF 2007, Banxico 2008). The main issues relate to lack of independence of regulators, that can introduce regulatory forbearance, lack of consolidated supervision of conglomerates, and stronger regulation of development banks. High net interest margins and operating

Figure 1.8. **Business and consumer confidence**

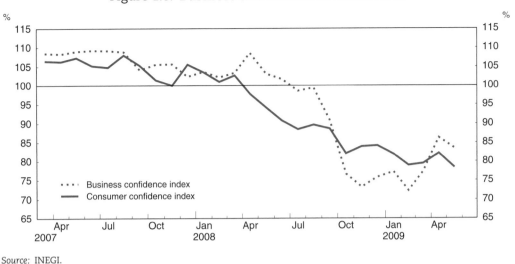

Source: INEGI.

StatLink ⬛🖳 http://dx.doi.org/10.1787/683476487586

costs provide some cushion for absorbing losses. However, the financial indicators tend to be backward looking and can change rapidly as the economy worsens. The main risk is likely to be credit risks. These are likely to be highest in banks with important exposure to consumer credit to marginal clients – the search for higher yield had led some banks to grant credit to customers without credit history (Banxico 2008). The exposure by banks to the sovereign can also affect asset quality and risks, should lower oil revenues increase sovereign financing needs and reduce the price of government paper.

The weakening economy and declining asset prices could, however, generate second-round effects on Mexican banks with a feedback effect on the real economy. If the economic and financial conditions further deteriorate, consumers and enterprises may find it difficult to service their debts, affecting banks' balance sheets. Coupled with the impact of declining asset prices on collateral and bank balance sheets, credit may shrink further. The rise in non-performing credit card loans to 10.3% of total in early 2009 is a first sign of potential problems. However, there has not been an explosive growth of the delinquency rate.

The near term outlook remains dim

Weighed down by adverse external developments and financial markets under stress, the economy is set to shrink in 2009 and recover only gradually in 2010 as the world and US economies improve (Table 1.2). Mexico's dependence on exports to the US market makes the outlook largely dependent on developments there. The depressed state of the US economy is reducing growth in Mexico substantially. Domestic consumption and investment will continue to slow down, influenced by rising unemployment and overall uncertainty on the outlook. In the past, real shocks in Mexico have tended to be long in duration (Box 1.1) potentially reflecting economic rigidities. Low productivity and declining oil production and prices are likely to remain drags on growth. Simulations with a VAR model (Box 1.2) point to a slow recovery. Inflation will come down as activity and world commodity prices remain low and monetary policy continues to keep expectations anchored. On the other hand, the current account has not experienced any significant

Table 1.2. **Forecasts for the Mexican economy**

Mexico: Demand, output and prices

	2005	2006	2007	2008	2009	2010
	Current prices MXN billion	Percentage changes, volume (2003 prices)				
Private consumption	6 139.0	5.7	3.9	1.6	−6.8	1.0
Government consumption	991.9	1.7	2.1	0.6	4.6	3.3
Gross fixed capital formation	1 867.1	9.8	7.2	5.0	−11.9	5.8
Final domestic demand	8 998.0	6.1	4.4	2.2	−6.8	2.2
Stockbuilding1	385.4	−0.3	−0.5	0.2	−1.5	0.5
Total domestic demand	9 383.4	5.7	3.8	2.3	−8.1	2.8
Exports of goods and services	2 505.6	11.0	5.6	1.5	−18.4	2.1
Imports of goods and services	2 639.6	12.7	7.0	4.5	−17.5	2.1
Net exports1	−134.0	−0.7	−0.6	−1.0	0.4	−0.1
GDP at market prices	9 249.5	5.1	3.3	1.4	−8.0	2.8
GDP deflator	–	6.7	4.5	6.6	3.6	3.4
Memorandum items						
Consumer price index	–	3.6	4.0	5.1	5.4	3.1
Private consumption deflator	–	3.4	4.8	6.9	7.7	3.2
Unemployment rate2	–	3.2	3.4	3.5	5.7	6.9
Current account balance3	–	−0.4	−0.8	−0.4	−0.4	−0.5

1. Contributions to changes in real GDP (percentage of real GDP in previous year), actual amount in the first column.
2. Based on National Employment Survey.
3. As a percentage of GDP.
Source: OECD Economic Outlook 85 database.

Box 1.1. **What happens during recessions in Mexico and what can a recovery today look like?**

Mexico has had five major economic cycles over the past decades with recessions often preceded by overheating financial markets, collapses in oil prices, or a US economic downturn. Since 1980 there have been five cyclical troughs (1983Q2, 1986Q4, 1988Q2, 1995Q2, 2001Q4). Turning points are identified with an algorithm developed by Harding and Pagan (2002) and a recession is defined as the period from peak to trough.[1] A bust is a decline of more than 20% from peak to trough in credit, equity or oil prices, or a 5% decline in US industrial production. A recession in Mexico is associated with a bust when at the onset these aggregates exceeded the above thresholds. The recessions differ in their duration (peak/trough), in the length of the recovery (quarters to reach real GDP level in previous peak) and the real GDP loss (peak/trough). All severe recessions have been accompanied by a credit or equity price bust. In contrast to previous cycles, in 2000 and 2008 there were no fiscal or banking crises.

Table 1.3. **Recessions and busts in selected variables**

Onset of recession	Credit crunch	Equity price bust	Oil price bust	US industrial production bust
1982q1	1	0	0	1
1985q4	1	0	0	0
1988q1	0	1	0	0
1995q1	1	1	0	0
2000q4	1	1	1	1
2008q4	0	1	1	1

Source: OECD and IMF International Financial Statistics.

Box 1.1. **What happens during recessions in Mexico and what can a recovery today look like?** *(cont.)*

Figure 1.9. **Recessions in Mexico**[1]

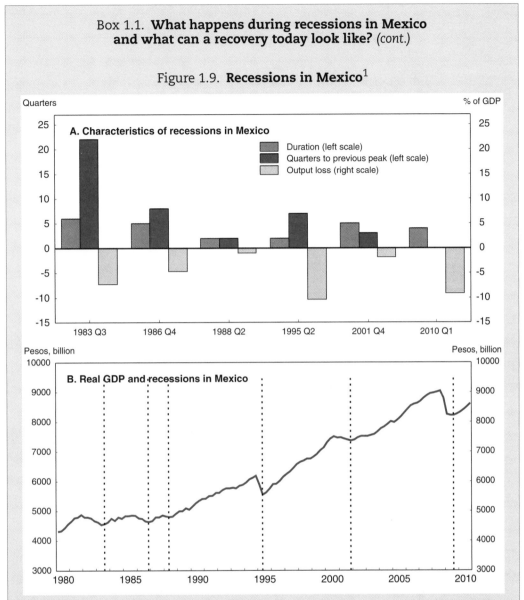

1. Turning points are identified using the Harding and Pagan (2002) methodology. Dates refer to cyclical troughs.

Source: OECD and IMF International Financial statistics.

StatLink ᘒ http://dx.doi.org/10.1787/683532708568

Recessions in Mexico have, in general, been accompanied by sharp declines in domestic demand, while exports have increased. Investment in particular has been severely influenced by credit market busts. The positive contribution of exports is likely to reflect large devaluations connected to recessions in Mexico. Recessions preceded by financial market turmoil have tended to have large output losses of up to 10% of GDP, while the length of recovery shows no clear pattern. However, the duration of the first and last recession in the sample, in which there were important real sector shocks, is longer.

Box 1.1. **What happens during recessions in Mexico and what can a recovery today look like?** (cont.)

Table 1.4. **Recessions and losses in selected variables**

Onset of Recession	GDP	Duration	Private Consumption	Investment	Exports
1982q1	−7.2	6	−7.2	−41.4	35.1
1985q4	−4.7	5	−4.7	−18.5	12.9
1988q1	−1.0	2	−1.6	0.6	5.0
1995q1	−10.3	2	−12.3	−34.2	21.1
2000q4	−1.8	5	1.6	−8.7	−8.2
Average above	−5	4	−4.8	−20.5	13.1
2008Q4	−9.11	61	−7.9	−14.2	−22.2

Onset of Recession	Imports	Industrial Production	Oil price	Credit	Equity price
1982q1	−59.2	−14.1	−12.1	−46.5	n.a.
1985q4	−14.6	−10.0	−46.0	−24.4	172.3
1988q1	17.1	−1.0	−9.4		−18.6
1995q1	−18.6	−11.8	9.5	−20.0	−37.3
2000q4	−5.7	−5.5	−35.4	−17.2	−15.5
Average above	−16.2	−8.5	−18.7	−25.9	25.2
2008Q4	−22.6	n.a.	n.a.	n.a.	n.a.

Note: Peak-to-trough losses. 2008Q4 is based on OECD forecasts for Economic Outlook 85. Industrial production, oil prices, credit and equity prices used in the analysis are from the IMF International Financial Statistics and therefore no projections are made here.

If the past is any guide for the future the current recession will be longer than the 1995 Tequila crisis but similar to the 1983 debt crisis, while being less deep than either. In contrast to many of the past recessions the current financial crisis is mainly exogenous to Mexico and its improved fundamentals are mitigating its effects. It is driven mainly by real sector influences which can mean a lower output loss but a longer duration. In the past it was often exports that pulled Mexico out of a through. However, as this time the world is in recession it may take longer for Mexican exports to recover despite the beneficial impact of the depreciating currency.

1. A complete cycle lasts at least five quarters and the contraction or expansion phase at least two quarters. If peaks or troughs are non-alternating the, respectively, highest or lowest level of the non-alternating peaks or troughs is chosen as the turning point.

deterioration given the close link between Mexican imports and non-oil exports, the depreciation of the exchange rate and the contraction in demand.

The main risk to the Mexican economy is that the downturn in US activity will be deeper or last longer than projected, further affecting Mexico's exports and FDI. Although oil prices have recovered in 2009 so far, a prolonged downturn in the United States and the world economy could also imply a further reduction in oil prices, at the same time as Mexico's oil production and reserves are declining substantially, potentially jeopardizing fiscal objectives more than expected. In addition, market sentiment could turn further against emerging markets like Mexico, putting downward pressure on the peso. Rising unemployment can trigger fiscal pressures in an economy with large perceived

Box 1.2. **The impact of external shocks on the Mexican economy**

To assess potential effects of current external shocks on output, a VAR was estimated for Mexico. The methodology follows closely that in IMF (2009a). The included variables are US industrial production, US pending house sales, the international oil price, measured by the London Brent Crude index, international credit conditions, proxied by the VIX-index, and the bilateral exchange rate against the dollar. The model is estimated on quarterly growth rates, with four lags, from 1996 to 2008, and assumes that domestic variables have no effect on international or US variables.

The estimation shows that Mexican GDP is strongly affected by US factors, although initially domestic ones dominate. After one year the US variables take over domestic ones, and explain almost half of the variance after eight quarters. US industrial production explains about a third of the forecast variation after 8 quarters, which is similar in magnitude to idiosyncratic shocks. The conditions in the US housing market also have a significant impact, especially over time. This reflects the increasing vertical integration of production chains across the Mexican – US border in high yield industries, and the large number of Mexicans working in both manufacturing and housing sectors in the United States. Variation in oil prices explain 17 per cent of the variation in GDP after 8 quarters, reflecting the importance of oil revenues in public consumption. Credit conditions explain less, but are clearly significant and increase over time. The exchange rate effect is small – it explains only 3 percent after eight quarters.

The results point to a slow recovery from external shocks. Mexico will be adversely hit by the US downturn and the deterioration of the US housing market, and it will take some time for these shocks to go through the economy. In addition, the drop in oil prices and tightening of credit conditions will have a contractionary effect on the economy. The strong depreciation of the peso would moderate the impact of these shocks only slightly. The model indicates that a shock to US industrial production will be transmitted to the Mexican economy by more than 50 per cent after one quarter, and by more than 80 per cent after four quarters.

Table 1.5. **Variance decomposition of shocks to Mexican GDP (%), 8 quarters forward**

Quarters forward	US factors		other factors		Mexican GDP	USD/peso exchange rate
	US industrial production	US housing market conditions	London Oil price index	VIX-index		
1	4.7	5.6	16.2	3.4	69.8	0
2	34.9	3.4	11.4	2.4	46.6	1.0
3	36.6	6.9	16.6	3.3	35.3	1.0
4	33.1	11.5	15.6	4.7	33.5	1.2
5	32.2	11.2	15.2	5.5	32.8	2.8
6	30.6	14.1	15.8	5.4	30.9	3.0
7	29.3	14.0	17.6	6.0	29.6	3.2
8	28.8	14.2	17.4	6.2	30.0	3.1

Box 1.2. **The impact of external shocks on the Mexican economy** (cont.)

Figure 1.10. **Impulse response functions to Mexican GDP from external shocks**

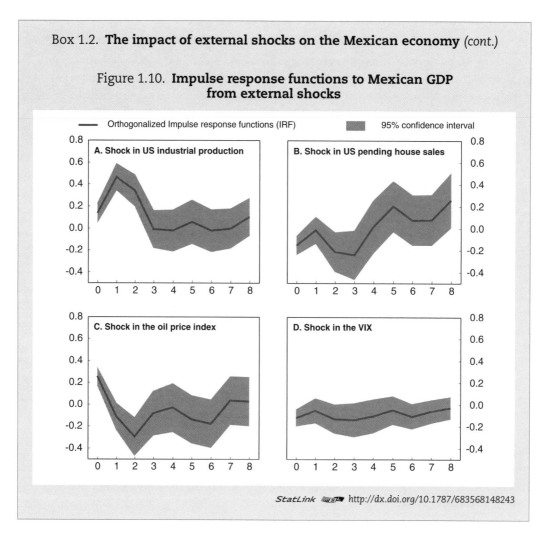

StatLink http://dx.doi.org/10.1787/683568148243

inequalities, further affecting stability and recovery prospects. This reinforces the need to shift more of the stimulus to sustain employment and incomes of the moderately poor.

External financing may be another risk over time if conditions for emerging markets worsen further. The IMF estimated gross external financing requirements in 2009 of about USD 82 billion (IMF 2009b), which the government expects will be met comfortably by private inflows and increases in public sector liabilities to multilateral lenders (IDB, World Bank). Nonetheless, as a result of the downturn in economic activity, the current account deficit to be financed has decreased. A cushion for these risks is obtained by using the credit line with the US Federal Reserve and the IMF Flexible Credit Line (FCL). The former was already activated in April to auction credit for about USD 5 billion. Depending on the prevailing conditions in international financial markets, these risks may continue in 2010.

Another risk is that banks' creditors will be unable to pay. Although the banking sector seems sound and has room to absorb shocks, a sharp deterioration in portfolios' as the economy worsens could trigger problems with bank balance sheets. This would further affect confidence, the availability of credit and the timing and strength of the rebound from the crisis.

The impact of the economic downturn on the real sector

The real sector started to feel the pain of the crisis towards end 2008, led by dropping exports (Figure 1.11). Non-oil exports began to fall sharply in October 2008, which intensified already decelerating manufacturing output, even though substantial depreciation in the real effective exchange rate in recent months has significantly raised Mexico's competitiveness. The car industry, a major export earner, has been hit particularly hard by a slowdown in US consumer demand, while textiles are losing market share to Asian competitors. The drop in exports may have been intensified by adjustments in global inventories in manufacturing (IMF 2009c). Exports are also being affected by the sharply declining oil production and prices, which intensified towards end-2008.

Figure 1.11. **Export and production recent developments**

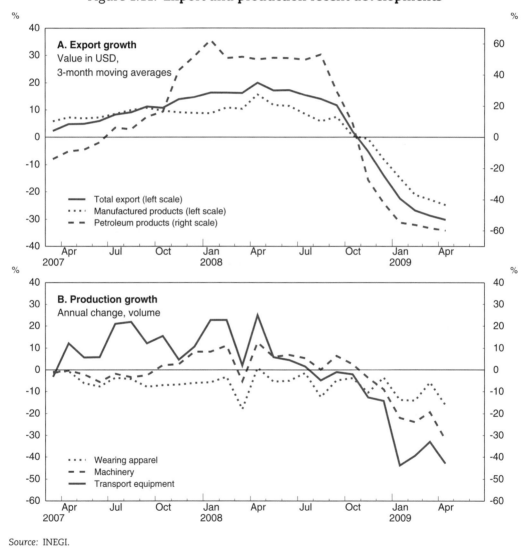

Source: INEGI.

StatLink ᴍᴚᴘ *http://dx.doi.org/10.1787/683607777524*

The rise in unemployment and worsened expectations are being felt in lower consumer demand and confidence (see Figure 1.8). As a result, the downturn spread to the service sector towards end-2008. Business confidence reached the lowest level for 15 years in January 2009, which is reflected in investment falling away. The only dynamic component of demand has been public expenditure. For example, budgetary allocations for investment increased by over 17% in real terms in 2008. However, the construction sector has still contracted due to a very sharp reduction in private investment.

Inflation pressures persisted in 2008 despite the decline in world commodity prices and the slowing of Mexican activity, but have gradually eased in 2009. Nonetheless, inflation, has been resilient and has been above the target rate more than 300 basis points on average. The sharp rise in inflation in 2008 above the central bank's target rate was largely due to first and second-round effects of supply shocks from commodity prices (Figure 1.12). Demand and wage pressures were subdued in 2008. While core inflation has remained persistent, non-core inflation started to show some levelling off in early 2009, driven by administered prices which account for about 17% of the CPI. In addition, within core inflation, that of services, which has typically been more rigid, has come down in an important way which is a positive development from the point of view of medium term inflation. However, prices of food and various consumer goods continued to rise, influenced by the lagged second-round effects of high commodity prices and rising tradables prices.

Figure 1.12. **Contribution to inflation**

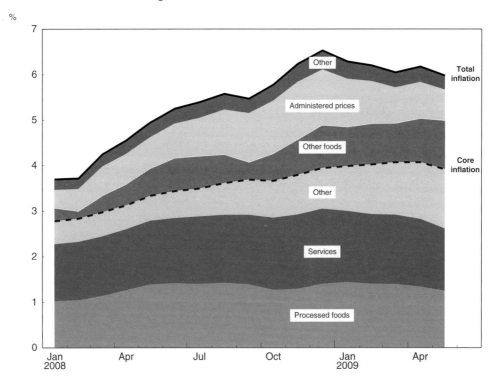

Source: Banco de México.

StatLink ᕼᑎᔕᑭ http://dx.doi.org/10.1787/683614633206

The pass-through from the exchange rate to prices is small partly reflecting the increasing credibility of the inflation-targeting framework implemented in 1999 (see Box 1.3). The pass-through may also have been reduced by the change in the nature of shocks, which have shifted from monetary to real ones since the adoption of the inflation targeting framework. However, the near-term pass-through might strengthen, if the recent

Box 1.3. **Exchange rate pass-through**

The standard approach to estimating the pass-through from the exchange rate to CPI inflation while controlling for domestic inflation determinants is the single-equation model proposed by Campa and Goldberg (2005).

$$\Delta \ln cpi_t = \alpha + \sum_{k=0}^{12} \beta_k \Delta \ln e_{t-k} + \sum_{k=0}^{12} \gamma_k \Delta \ln p_{t-k}^* + \sum_{k=0}^{12} \lambda_k gap_{t-k} + \varepsilon_t \qquad (1)$$

cpi_t is the consumer price index, α the intercept, e_t a nominal effective exchange rate index, p_t^* an index of foreign producer prices, gap_t the output gap and ε_t the regression residual. All data are from national sources or from the OECD and in monthly frequencies.[1] The output gap is calculated as the deviation of the logarithm of industrial production from its long term trend (obtained through a HP filter). In this specification, domestic CPI inflation is assumed to depend on nominal exchange rate movements, changes in the (foreign currency) prices of imports, and changes in aggregate demand.

The estimation of the model by rolling regressions of 8 years starting in 1990m1 shows that exchange rate pass-through in Mexico was strong at the beginning of the 1990s: a depreciation of the nominal exchange rate of 10% was passed through to an increase in the domestic consumer price index of around 4% after 12 months. After the adoption of the inflation targeting regime in 1999, the pass-through becomes insignificant. This is in line with the literature that argues that credibility gains from the adoption of inflation targeting help keep inflation expectations low following depreciations (see, for instance, Schmidt-Hebbel and Werner, 2002). Another explanation may be that the nature of shocks hitting the Mexican economy changed after 1999. While in the 1990s the Mexican economy was hit mainly by monetary shocks, after 1999 negative real shocks may have dampened the pass-through from the exchange rate to domestic prices through their negative effect on aggregate demand. The estimated effect of the output gap on inflation is insignificant throughout the sample period. This is consistent with studies estimating backward looking Phillips curves for Mexico (Ramos-Francia and Torres García, 2006), and is related to Mexico having faced several crises with high inflation and strongly negative output gaps over the sample period.

Against the background of the current economic crisis, it is crucial to keep credibility of monetary policy to maintain this reduced pass-through from the exchange rate to domestic prices to keep some leeway to monetary policy. The pass-through estimates for the period 1999-2008, suggest that only a small fraction of the recent depreciation would be passed on to domestic prices. Inflation expectations in line with the Central Bank's target suggest that the recent depreciation did not tarnish the Central Bank's credibility.

Estimated coefficients

	1990-1998	1999-2008
$\sum_{k=0}^{12} \beta_k$	0.410*** (0.064)	0.010 (0.048)
$\sum_{k=0}^{12} \gamma_k$	1.724*** (0.328)	0.052 (0.120)
$\sum_{k=0}^{12} \lambda_k$	−0.045 (0.027)	0.001 (0.012)

Note: *** statistically significant at 1%. Standard deviations in parentheses.

Box 1.3. **Exchange rate pass-through** (cont.)

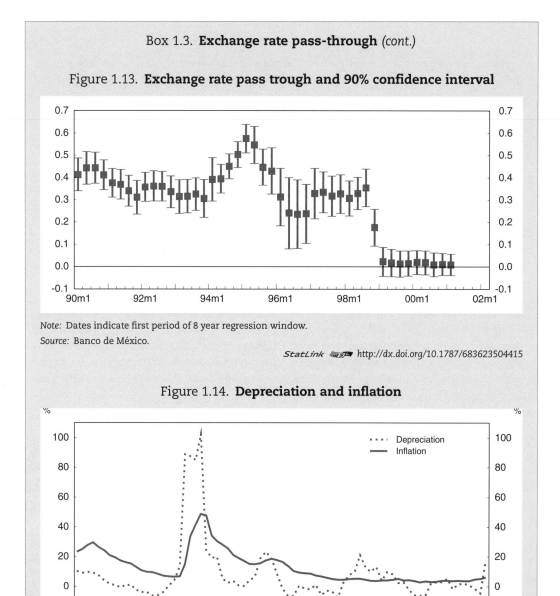

Figure 1.13. **Exchange rate pass trough and 90% confidence interval**

Note: Dates indicate first period of 8 year regression window.

Source: Banco de México.

StatLink ᴍᴤᴘ http://dx.doi.org/10.1787/683623504415

Figure 1.14. **Depreciation and inflation**

Note: Year-on-year growth rate of nominal effective exchange rate and CPI.

Source: OECD, Analytical database.

StatLink ᴍᴤᴘ http://dx.doi.org/10.1787/683641155720

1. Mexican CPI and nominal effective exchange rate are from OECD sources, the foreign producer price index is the US producer price index for finished goods from the Bureau of Labour Statistics and Mexican industrial production is from INEGI. All data are seasonally adjusted using the Census Bureau X12 programme and the first differenced series have been tested for stationarity.

changes in the peso dollar rate are perceived to be permanent. Expectations for higher than targeted inflation in 2009 remain above the target zone of 2-4%, while those for the longer term remain close to the upper bound (Figure 1.15) pointing to relatively high credibility of the inflation targeting framework. At the same time, the large change in the exchange rate can increase risk of unanchoring expectations.

Figure 1.15. **Inflation expectations**

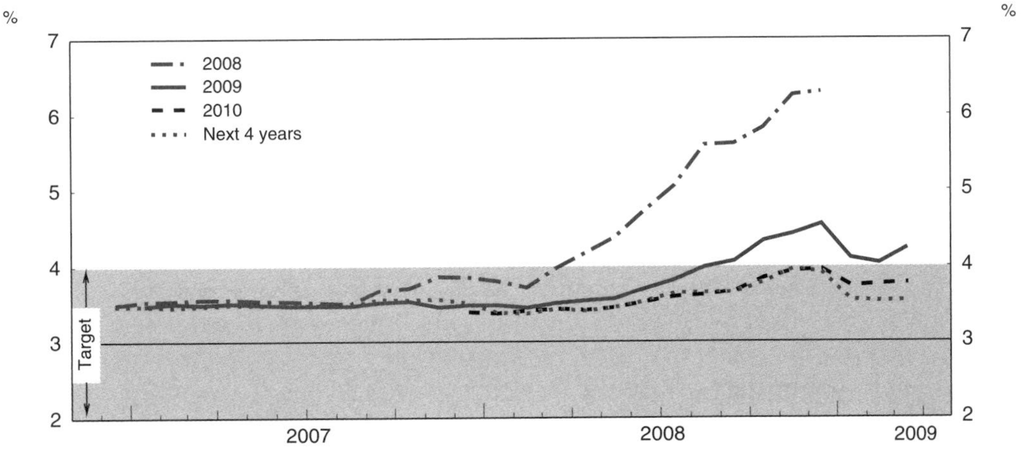

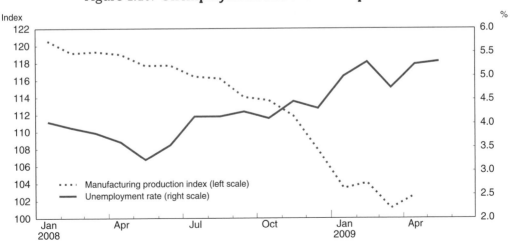

Source: Banco de México.

StatLink ᵃˢᵖ http://dx.doi.org/10.1787/683674256650

Adverse labour market impact

The declining activity is being reflected with some lag in worsening labour market outcomes. Employment in the formal sector started to decline rapidly towards end-2008, especially in construction and manufacturing (Figure 1.16), although some of the unemployed are absorbed by the informal sector. Nevertheless, the pace of job losses seems to be diminishing as in other countries. The rise in unemployment began in mid-2008 and has intensified recently despite measures to maintain jobs in the government's anti-crisis package. Some buffer to the employment situation is given by the rigid labour laws that make dismissals expensive and the broadly stable employment in the government sector. Further pressures on the labour market are likely to come from an expected return of migrants from the United States suffering from the slump in construction and other activity there. Unemployment in the United States among Hispanics at end-2008 was rising rapidly

Figure 1.16. **Unemployment and industrial production**

1. Three-month moving averages.

Source: INEGI.

StatLink ᵃˢᵖ http://dx.doi.org/10.1787/683716468440

and at 12% is higher than average (Pew Hispanic Center, 2009). Real wage growth in Mexico has been sluggish and even negative recently. This trend may continue further in the current market situation, dampening disposable incomes and consumption. The poor are better protected now than during the 1995 crisis, but the moderately poor are vulnerable owing to the lack of broader social safety nets (Box 1.4).

Box 1.4. **Protecting the poor during the crisis**

Protection of the poorest has improved substantially since the 1995 crisis but safety nets for the moderately poor remain small. Government spending on social programmes (*Desarrollo Social* budget category) is currently more than double in real terms than in 1995 (Figure 1.17) at the onset of the Tequila crisis. The targeting of poverty reduction programmes has also improved, which has contributed to a decline in poverty (Figure 1.17), and should ease the impact of the crisis on the poorest segments of the population. The government is also controlling prices of selected foodstuffs consumed by the poor.

Figure 1.17. **Social spending and poverty levels**

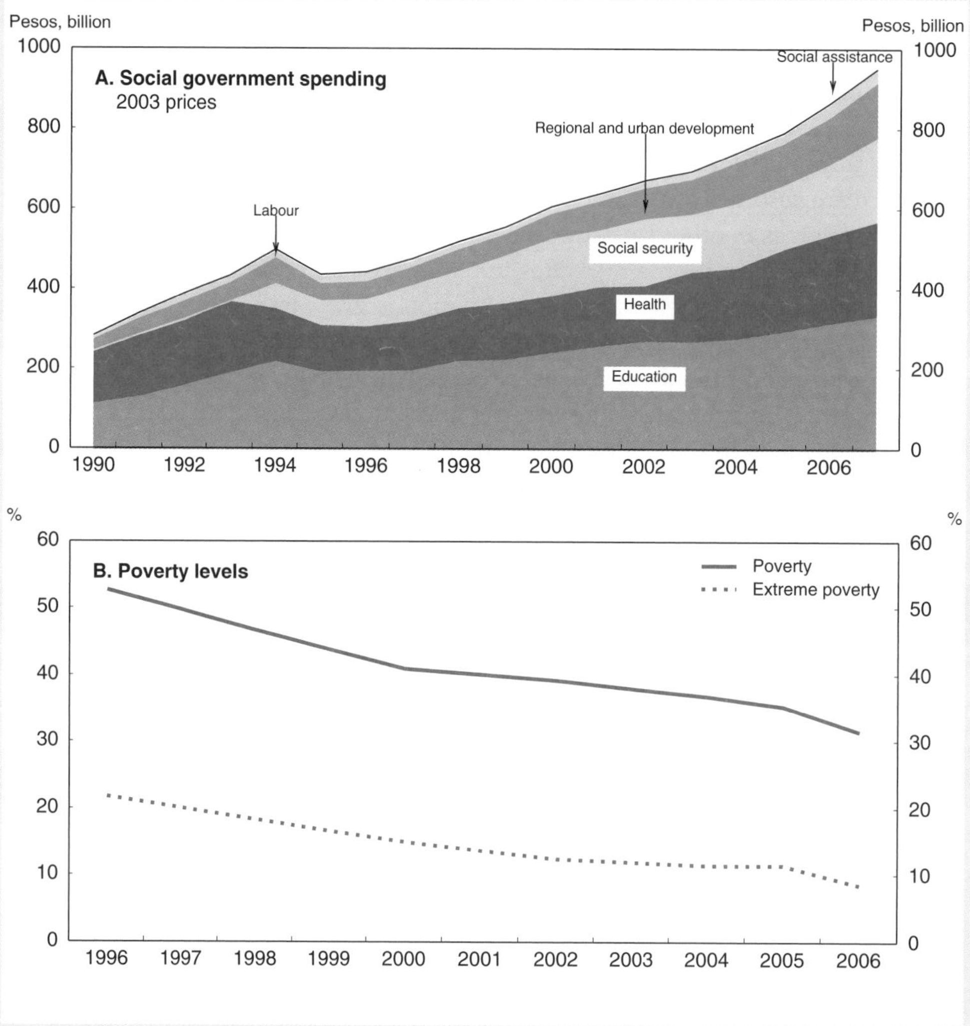

Source: ECLAC and Anexo Estadístico del Segundo Informe del Gobierno.

StatLink ⟲ http://dx.doi.org/10.1787/683748452240

Box 1.4. **Protecting the poor during the crisis** *(cont.)*

However, the moderately poor lack social protection. Social security provides health and pension benefits for formal sector employees when employed, and there are limited unemployment benefits for those individuals with individual retirement accounts. Through the shedding of formal sector jobs, the current crisis is likely to result in an increase in the number of families that are neither covered by targeted poverty reduction programmes nor by social security benefits. Their disposable incomes are further affected by the higher than average inflation in the basic consumer basket. Remittances from abroad help sustain incomes in some areas.

The main poverty reduction programmes should be protected during the crisis:

- The *Oportunidades* programme provides means-tested conditional cash transfers to low-income families conditional on children's regular school attendance and provision with a basic health package. It covered about 5 million families in 2008 with positive effects on school attendance and health, in particular of girls (Todd and Wolpin, 2006, Schultz, 2004).

- The *Seguro Popular* provides a voluntary health insurance for people without access to social security. It covered about 8 million mainly low-income families in 2008 and has been shown to have reduced the incidence of high health spending among the poor.

- The *Procampo* programme, a part of the *Programa Especial Concurrente* of over 100 rural support programmes was introduced in 1993 to compensate farmers with cash subsidies for the elimination of input subsidies, price support and import protection as a result of Mexico's entry into NAFTA. In 2007 it covered 2.4 million beneficiary farmers, mainly at the lower end of the income distribution.

The social safety net for the moderately poor should be reinforced to avoid these families falling into extreme poverty. The government's anti-crisis package contains measures for temporary employment programmes, job maintenance and extending health coverage for the unemployed by some months. However, the amounts devoted to these programmes (6 mmp) are small compared to, for example, support to maintain energy prices low (50 mmp) that also benefit the higher income deciles (see Figure 1.21) or investment (30mmp). One way to protect these families is to shift more of the anti-crisis spending to temporary employment programmes.

The macroeconomic policy mix is getting more coherent

The financial turmoil and economic downturn are putting Mexico's policy mix to a new test. Although macroeconomic policies were broadly prudent over the past decade, their timing and mix may have aggravated economic cycles. The combination of a tightening monetary policy, and a pro-cyclical, expansionary fiscal policy in an environment of booming commodity prices may not have been the best combination to contain inflationary pressures. Policies became, however, better synchronised towards end 2008, when both fiscal and monetary stances started to loosen in the wake of weakening activity. The government's anti-inflation tool kit also included controls on administered prices, in particular gasoline, which are set through a smoothing mechanism.

Monetary policy

Policy rates had increased gradually until August 2008 to keep inflation expectations anchored, before the easing cycle that began in January 2009 as the balance of risks deteriorated significantly more on economic activity than on the inflation outlook. To contain inflation expectations in 2008, the central bank hiked policy rates in three consecutive moves to 8.25%. As price pressures started to show signs of levelling off in early 2009, policy rates were lowered in several steps to 4.50% in July. The initial pace of monetary easing was cautious reflecting risk for capital outflows and further pressures on the exchange rate and thereby on prices. At the same time, monetary conditions have been eased by the depreciation of the peso (Figure 1.18).

Figure 1.18. **Monetary conditions index**

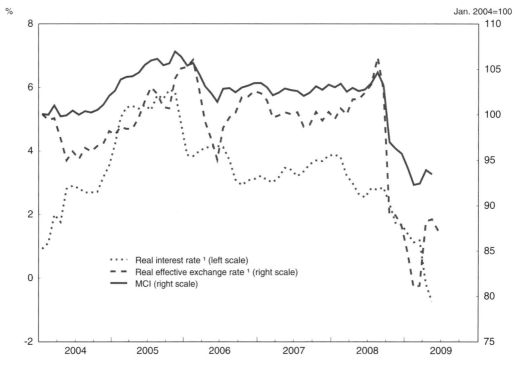

1. Using consumer price index.
Source: OECD and Banco de México.

StatLink ᵃᵍᵈ⁵ http://dx.doi.org/10.1787/683810014116

The monetary stance of Banxico has been broadly appropriate. The central bank has been successful in containing longer-term inflation expectations, which is the main channel of transmission in an economy with low financial deepening.[6] Furthermore, its monetary policy stance has resulted in positive real interest rates in recent years, in contrast to many emerging and industrial countries, which is likely to have helped contain excessive credit growth, reducing vulnerability to shocks. The moderate easing of monetary conditions since October 2008 brought about by the peso depreciation and the cutting of policy rates since January, was welcome in view of the rapidly declining activity. However, this has not translated into lower real interest rates for all private borrowers as higher risk premiums have at times offset lower policy rates. A further deterioration of economic activity in Mexico might give some room for further lowering of policy rates to sustain demand, provided expectations remain anchored, especially as more support from fiscal policy is limited (see below), unless external conditions are set to worsen further (see below). The estimated weak exchange-rate pass-through could limit risks to price stability.

A simple Taylor rule simulation, that takes account of the output gap and small deviations from the inflation target but does not account for the effects on capital flows and the exchange rate, suggests that policy rates should have been somewhat higher and increased earlier in 2008, and have been lowered a bit faster in early 2009 (Figure 1.19).

Figure 1.19. **Taylor-rule interest rates**

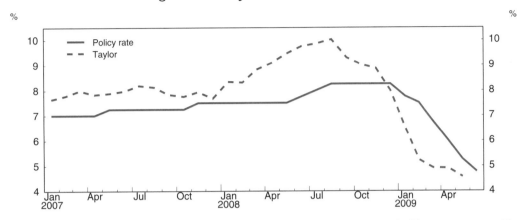

Note: Estimated on monthly data starting January 2000, with the output gap smoothed between quarters. The estimations suggest coefficients for CPI at 1.1 and for the output gap at 0.5.

StatLink ⟶ http://dx.doi.org/10.1787/683825772253

Macro-prudential measures

Measures by the financial authorities to ease liquidity in some markets and boost confidence have helped smooth the initial impact of the 2008 financial turmoil. The establishment of a swap facility with the US Federal Reserve, increased liquidity in domestic markets, and government guarantees for loans have helped confidence in the financial markets. The central bank and the banking commission are also closely following developments in banks in terms of capital adequacy and quality of credit portfolios as the slowdown starts to affect the real sector. The authorities should be ready to take measures to support solvent banks if the situation worsens. The moderate leverage and low exposure to complex foreign or domestic financial products should limit risks of large asset write downs.

As the pressure on the peso intensified again in February 2009, the central bank started to intervene by selling some of its international reserves directly in the foreign exchange markets. Between October 2008 and February 2009 interventions amounted to about USD 19 billion, bringing reserves down to USD 80 billion or 7% of GDP. While this remains comfortable, it is below the stocks accumulated by many other emerging markets. In April Mexico drew on the US Fed credit line to increase dollar liquidity to help private enterprises rollover dollar debt. These measures, and the establishment of the USD 47 billion FLC with the IMF have contributed to calm down financial markets and stabilized the exchange rate. In turn, this has led to a significant reduction in the amount of reserves that have been sold in the foreign exchange market. While further depreciation can make it more difficult to lower interest rates, Mexico should continue letting the exchange rate adjust if the pressures reflect a change in fundamentals, such as further capital outflows and worsening economic outlook.

Fiscal policy

Fiscal policy has been broadly prudent but at times pro-cyclical. A pro-cyclical fiscal policy is common in many emerging markets and often reflects concern for solvency, difficulties in funding deficits in recessions, and political constraints in managing spending in good times (Schmidt-Hebbel 2008, Perry *et al.* 2008) While much of this applies to Mexico, pro-cyclicality is also created by a balanced budget rule. The balanced budget rule, which applies to part of the Mexican fiscal deficit, is by construction pro-cyclical in terms of the budgets that are approved—the more you collect the more you spend (Box 1.5). In countries with volatile resource revenues this can lead to large swings in spending. On the other hand, Mexico has tried to reduce spending volatility by a rule that transfers higher-than-expected oil revenues to stabilisation funds. However, balances in the funds are capped at low levels creating a bias for spending large oil revenues (see Chapter 2). For example, a significant amount of excess revenues in 2008, which were about 4.4% of GDP higher than budgeted, were spent as savings in the stabilisation funds increased only by

---

Box 1.5. **Defining the fiscal balance and fiscal stance in Mexico**

The fiscal balance. The fiscal balance in Mexico is composed of the traditional budget (budget) plus lending operations (net lending or public sector borrowing requirements). The traditional budget, which in recent years has been subject to a balanced budget rule, includes non-oil revenues, oil revenues (royalties), Pemex revenues, overall expenditures, and current Pemex spending. Lending operations are added to the balance of the budget to obtain the total fiscal balance (or deficit). Apart from Pemex investment (until 2009), lending operations include *e.g.* transfers to development banks. As of 2009 Pemex investment was shifted within the total deficit from lending operations to the traditional budget. However, the balanced budget rule is now calculated without the Pemex investment.

Fiscal stance. The measurement of underlying and cyclical components of the fiscal balance in Mexico is complicated by the volatility of the oil price. One measure of the underlying balance is a cyclically adjusted total fiscal balance that includes the oil economy. The cyclical components includes oil revenues that deviate from an estimated trend price of oil (HP filter), cyclical non-oil revenues (income elasticity of 1.05), non-recurrent revenues and the gasoline price support that maintains prices constant in real terms. The change in this balance (change in the non-cyclical component of the deficit) measures the impulse from the fiscal stance to the economy. An alternative measure of the fiscal stance is the non-oil underlying fiscal balance, which excludes oil revenues (Pemex and royalties and Pemex expenditures and the gasoline price support, and the cyclical component of non-oil revenues). Both measures have moved in the same direction, with the non-oil balance having slightly larger swings in recent years (Figure 1.20, Table 1.6).

The Mexican fiscal stance has also been measured by a change in the nominal fiscal deficit with and without non-recurring revenues. For example, IMF 2009c defines Mexican fiscal stance in 2009 as the change in the deficit from 2008 with no account for cyclical factors. The government also tends to measure the change in the nominal deficit as a measure of its fiscal policy stance. This explains at times different numbers and interpretations given to the stance of policy in different documents.

To facilitate fiscal policy analysis Mexico should start reporting its fiscal accounts to the OECD under international rules in line with other members.

Box 1.5. **Defining the fiscal balance and fiscal stance in Mexico** (*cont.*)

Table 1.6. **Mexico – Components of cyclically adjusted fiscal balances, 2004-2010, % of potential GDP**

	2003	2004	2005	2006	2007	2008	2009* Proj.	2010** Proj.
Underlying balance	–3.3	–2.1	–0.8	–0.8	–1.4	–3.2	–3.2	–2.4
non-oil revenues	13.5	12.3	13.5	13.7	13.8	14.2	13.9	12.8
oil revenues	6.2	6.9	7.8	8.3	8.8	8.6	8.4	8.0
expenditure	23.1	21.3	22.1	22.8	24.0	26.1	25.5	23.2
(*of which* Pemex)	2.7	2.9	2.7	3.0	2.9	2.7	3.1	2.6
Non-oil underlying balance	–6.8	–6.1	–5.9	–6.1	–7.3	–9.2	–8.5	–7.8
Oil underlying balance		4.0	5.1	5.3	5.9	5.9	5.3	5.4
change in non-oil und. balance		–0.7	–0.2	0.2	1.2	1.9	–0.7	–0.7
change in underlying balance		–1.2	–1.3	0.0	0.5	1.9	0.0	–0.7

* Potential output is estimated with the production function method, "permanent" oil revenues with a HP filtered net oil revenues series, gasoline price support is cyclical spending, non-oil tax revenues have 1.05 elasticity to income. Non-recurring revenues and one-off transfers to funds excluded from the und. balance except investment spending.
** Assumes no measures taken to compensate for lower expected oil and non-oil revenues and that expenditure remains broadly constant as share of GDP. 2009 assumes one-off income from central bank profits and the oil funds of about 1% of GDP; 2010 assumes one-off revenue of about 0.5% of GDP from oil funds. Revenues from the oil hedge in 2009 are included in oil revenues.
Source: SHCP, OECD staff calculations.

about 0.5% of GDP. Nevertheless, the use of stabilization funds allows for some counter-cyclical compensation when revenues in a fiscal year are lower than budgeted. On the other hand, fiscal prudence stemming from the balanced budget rule has enabled a sharp decline in public debt in an environment of strong growth. This has created fiscal space for additional spending in downturns provided it can be financed.

The balanced budget rule in an environment of booming commodity prices led to a positive fiscal impulse in 2007 and 2008 despite economic growth being above potential (Figure 1.20) until mid-2008. After improving until 2006, the estimated structural deficit

Figure 1.20. **Mexico: Fiscal stance 2003-2010**

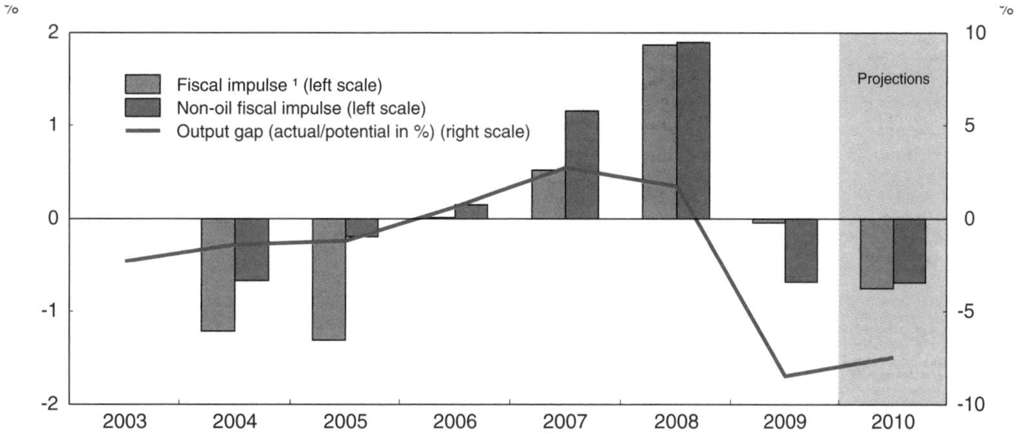

1. Change in the cyclically adjusted fiscal balance (% of GDP).
Source: SHCP and OECD.

StatLink http://dx.doi.org/10.1787/683861581112

started to worsen, culminating at about 3% of GDP in 2008 with an estimated impulse of about 1.9% of GDP to demand (Table 1.7, Figure 1.20). The trend is similar for the non-oil structural balance. While structural revenues remained relatively constant in terms of potential GDP, expenditures increased as most of the higher-than-expected oil revenues were spent (Table 1.6). The cyclical component was driven by the sharp rise in oil revenues. Apart from oil-related items, automatic stabilisers in Mexico are estimated to be small and mainly relate to non-oil tax revenues. Moreover, even though energy subsidies and the mechanism for smoothing gasoline prices in 2008 may have supported activity as it started to decline towards mid-2008, it goes against the government's overall fiscal objectives of reinforcing investment and social spending. Saving more of the revenues or spending them, for example, on investment in social programmes over time could have had a more lasting impact on the welfare of the Mexicans (structural fiscal issues are discussed in more detail in Chapter 2).

Table 1.7. **Mexico: Fiscal indicators (% of GDP)**

	2003	2004	2005	2006	2007	2008	2009 proj.***	2010** proj.***
Traditional budget	−0.6	−0.2	−0.1	0.1	0.0	0.0	−2.0	−3.6
Lending operations	−1.7	−0.2	−1.0	−0.4	−0.8	−1.0	−2.1	−1.2
Fiscal balance (with non-recurrent rev.)	−2.4	−0.4	−1.1	−0.3	−0.7	−1.0	−4.2	−4.8
Underlying balance*	−3.3	−2.1	−0.8	−0.8	−1.4	−3.2	−3.2	−2.4
Non-oil underlying balance	−6.8	−6.1	−5.9	−6.1	−7.3	−9.2	−8.5	−7.8
Cyclical component (Fiscal balance-und.balance)	1.0	1.7	−0.2	0.6	0.6	2.2	−1.0	−2.4
from								
oil rev. (gross)	−2.1	0.1	−0.5	0.0	−0.4	2.2	0.4	−0.3
non-oil rev.	0.3	1.1	0.1	0.4	1.0	0.8	−0.4	−0.9
oil price support and oil funds	−0.1	−0.5	−0.2	−0.1	0.0	0.8	0.7	0.0
Fiscal impulse (change in the underlying balance)		−1.2	−1.3	0.0	0.5	1.9	0.0	−0.7
(change in the non-oil underlying balance)		−0.7	−0.2	0.2	1.2	1.9	−0.7	−0.7
Automatic stabilizers (change in the cyclical balance) and discretionary spending		0.7	−1.9	0.8	0.1	1.6	−3.2	−1.4
Memo:								
Output gap (actual/potential in %)	−2.3	−1.4	−1.2	0.6	2.7	1.7	−8.5	−7.5
Tax/subsidy on gasoline (%of GDP)	1.2	0.6	0.2	−0.4	−0.4	−1.8	0.0	0.0
Fiscal balance (net of non-rec rev.)	−3.0	−1.8	−1.3	−0.6	−1.3	−1.5	−6.1	−4.8

* Potential output is estimated with the production function method, "permanent" oil revenues with a HP filtered net oil revenues series, gasoline price support is cyclical spending, non-oil tax revenues have 1.05 elasticity to income. Non-recurring revenues and one-off transfers to funds excluded from the und. balance except investment spending.
** Assumes no measures taken to compensate for lower expected oil and non-oil revenues and that expenditure remains broadly constant as share of GDP.
*** 2009 assumes one-off income from central bank profits and the oil funds of about 1% of GDP; 2010 assumes one-off revenue of about 0.5% of GDP from oil funds. Revenues from the oil hedge in 2009 are included in oil revenues.
Source: SHCP, OECD staff calculations.

The fiscal deficits are set to increase in the near future. In 2009 revenues are likely to decline as activity and oil prices fall, while spending increases in terms of GDP. Within spending, there are important increases in infrastructure outlays and support to development banks (about 0.7% of GDP) to help deal with the economic crisis and boost growth in the longer run, which are compensated by lower transfers and one-off revenues from central bank profits and the oil funds. The impulse from discretionary measures, measured as the change in the underlying deficit (OECD definition), to the economy would, however, be small as the structural deficit remains roughly unchanged. This is because spending is assumed to remain constant in terms of a lower nominal GDP, which actually implies that it declines compared to potential in line with the growing output gap. Assuming no corrective measures, the deficit for 2010 is estimated to worsen further as oil and other revenues drop along with activity. The authorities are planning to use the savings in the oil stabilisation funds to finance for part of the deficit.

The authorities also introduced an additional stimulus package in January 2009 to deal with the crisis, but within the existing budget to keep with the balanced budget rule. The measures amount to about 0.9% of GDP to be financed by revenue gains from peso depreciation and expected (one-off) profits from the central bank (0.8% of GDP). The 2009 budget and the package announced in early 2009 contain some welcome, timely, temporary and targeted measures such as time-bound employment subsidies, income support for the poorest and subsidies to credit in small and medium enterprises. As these groups are likely to be credit constrained, the measures may be effective in boosting demand. The increase in infrastructure spending is also welcome, although its impact is likely to be felt slowly due to implementation bottlenecks. However, maintaining price distortions in gasoline and electricity to households, raise issues with efficiency, equity and targeting. For example, two-thirds of gasoline and half of electricity are purchased by the three highest income groups (Figure 1.21), who are more likely to save the additional income. Targeting more measures at lower-income, credit constrained consumers would increase multiplier effects (see Box 1.6).

Figure 1.21. **Spending in energy by income deciles, 2006**

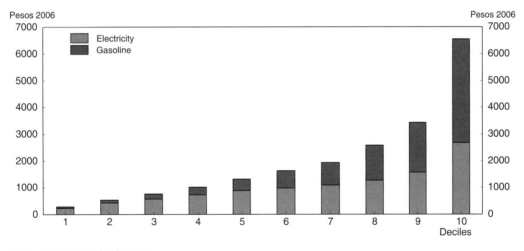

Source: ENIGH Household survey.

StatLink 🔗 http://dx.doi.org/10.1787/683875845443

Rising near-term fiscal risks limit room for further discretionary stimulus in 2009, thus putting more pressure on monetary policy. As the recession and low oil prices are likely to continue beyond 2009, Mexico's public debt and fiscal stance will come under increasing stress. The small savings in the stabilization fund, the end of the oil hedge (total net exports of hydrocarbons in 2009 are hedged at USD 70 per barrel) and uncertainties of future oil prices will put a pressure on revenues going forward when access to debt financing is likely to get costlier and more difficult. Higher deficits can then lead to a

Box 1.6. **The effectiveness of discretionary fiscal policy in Mexico**

Table 1.8. **The January 2009 fiscal package and special measures in the 2009 budget**

	bn pesos	in % of GDP
Additional energy price support	50.0	0.43
Temporary employment	5.0	0.04
Employment Programmes	2.0	0.02
Support to PEMEX suppliers	5.0	0.04
Additional infrastructure investment (mostly budget 2009)	85.0	0.74
Investment by PEMEX and States	30.0	0.26
Extension of healthcare benefits for the unemployed	5.0	0.04
Advance withdrawal of pensions for the unemployed	0.6	0.01
Subsidies to house improvements	7.4	0.06
Subsidies for environment-friendly appliances	0.8	0.01
Total	190.8	1.65

To be effective, discretionary fiscal policy should be timely, targeted and temporary.

Many of Mexico's measures are temporary and have a time limit. Employment subsidies and social transfers seem temporary, as, for example, the duration of additional health benefits and income transfers for the unemployed are limited. In contrast, energy price support is linked to oil price developments and has no clear sunset clauses. Infrastructure spending may imply a permanent increase of this item in the budget, which would, however, be justified by longer term fiscal objectives provided there is funding.

Structural factors and policy frameworks give moderate support for effectiveness of the stimuli in Mexico. The open capital account and flexible exchange rate tend to reduce the size of fiscal multipliers, while the shift in the monetary stance towards more accommodation should help fiscal policy effectiveness. It is also influenced by openness, potentially reducing the spillovers of public spending onto imports. The extent of the automatic stabilisers tends to reduce the effectiveness of discretionary fiscal actions. Apart from oil, they are small in Mexico reflecting both the small size of the public sector.

Summary of factors influencing the effectiveness of fiscal stimulus in Mexico

Macro	Overall assessment of macro factors: moderate	Structural	Overall assessment of structural factors: weak/ moderate	Fiscal	Overall assessment of fiscal factors: weak/ moderate
Clear threat of output shock	X	Spending productive		Low debt	X
Demand shock	X	Crowding out of private spending		Fiscal balance near equil.	X
Excess capacity	X	Lower taxes increase labour supply		Policy making quick	
Closed economy		Automatic stabilizers small	X	Reversed in good times	
Fixed exchange rate		Stimulus rapid effect		LT reforms being implemented	
Households liquidity const/ short horizons	X	Positive multipliers	X		
Expansion would not reduce confidence	X				
External stability					

X = applies to Mexico.

vicious circle of rise in real interest rates, financial market turmoil and adverse effects on the real economy. This reinforces caution on further discretionary stimuli and the importance of targeting the current one well.

At the same time, the 2010 budget should relax the balanced budget rule and let the "automatic stabilisers (including oil)" work to avoid excessive fiscal contraction. Following the rule would lead to a large contraction in demand in an environment of a large output gap. A moderate deficit can be achieved by letting revenues fall in line with demand while maintaining spending in nominal terms with some shifting of expenditures from energy price support to social transfers and employment maintenance. Despite the widening output gap the small size of government and automatic stabilizers would limit the increase in the deficit, provided spending remains under control. The current fiscal legal framework allows for some flexibility in relaxing the rule, which the government should use. Preliminary projections published by the authorities show a moderate increase in the deficit, which includes discretionary expansion by about 0.8% of GDP, financed by drawing down savings in the stabilization funds. Over time, a shift to a structural fiscal rule would remove the pro-cyclical bias and improve the fiscal policy framework by establishing structural countercyclical element in the budget (see Chapter 2).

Mexico also faces a number of daunting medium-term challenges, which should not be forgotten in the current crisis environment. Raising productivity and potential growth remain crucial for faster catch-up and require the pursuit of structural reform especially in the area of competition and rule of law. The emphasis on infrastructure spending in the stimulus package, if used efficiently, can help alleviate some infrastructure bottlenecks. Similarly, reducing inequalities is important for social peace and sustainability of pro-growth reforms. In this the efficiency of social spending is important to raise both education and health outcomes. Improving the efficiency and long-term growth potential of the oil sector, as a result of an adequate implementation of the Pemex reform, would also support fiscal sustainability and Mexico's growth potential. Reinforcing fiscal policy to support macroeconomic management and allocate resources to growth and social targets should support the structural reforms. Some of these challenges are dealt with in the OECD Going for Growth publication (2009) and following chapters.

Box 1.7. Key macroeconomic policy recommendations

Allow automatic fiscal stabilisers to play freely in 2009-10, but refrain from further discretionary stimulus

- Refrain from further stimulus in view of the potentially larger-than-expected deficit in 2009 and likely worsening of the fiscal outlook in 2010 (driven by lower oil and non-oil tax revenues in a slump). It may be difficult to finance a significantly larger fiscal deficit.

- Allow automatic stabilisers to operate freely in 2009-10. Draw down savings accumulated in the oil stabilisation fund.

- Shift spending in the fiscal stimulus package to targeted measures, such as temporary income support for the poor or employment subsidies. The government's decision not to lower taxes is welcome given the weaker multiplier effect and already narrow tax base.

- Protect social programs in the budget.

- Start reporting fiscal accounts to the OECD in ADB format.

> **Box 1.7. Key macroeconomic policy recommendations** *(cont.)*
>
> **There might be room for further lowering of policy rates**
>
> - If the outlook of economic activity deteriorates continue loosening of monetary policy, provided expectations remain anchored. Although the credit channel is weak, this can have an impact on confidence.
> - Continue to support credit with liquidity measures and general guarantees to development banks.
>
> **Monitor bank portfolios for impact of worsening outlook**
>
> - Monitor bank portfolios and rollover risks for enterprises with foreign credit carefully.

Notes

1. Capital market development was facilitated by creating the appropriate infrastructure and the increasing participation of institutional investors and mutual funds in domestic bond markets. The stock market is less developed with modest capitalization and dominated by a few large companies.

2. In 2008 Mexico's foreign debt was 15% of GDP, and short-term debt to reserves 10% compared to 40% and 610% in 1994 respectively before the Tequila crisis. In addition inflation in 1994 was in double digits and the current account was rapidly widening to 6-7% of GDP.

3. They intervened at the long end of the bond market, provided guarantees for commercial paper and borrowing, opened a swap arrangement with the US Federal Reserve and a credit facility with the IMF (Banxico).

4. Another 5% of GDP was directly from non-resident foreign banks.

5. Short term dollar positions are subject to liquidity requirements for less than 60 day positions; a regulation limits open positions in forex to 15% of capital (Banxico p. 64).

6. J. Sidaoui and M. Ramos Francia (2008) argue that the credit and interest channels are weak due to the low level and gradually expanding financial deepening in the economy (the credit to GDP ratio is about 20%).

Bibliography

Banxico (2008), Financial System Report 2007, Bank of Mexico.

Banxico (2009), Inflation Report October-December 2008, Bank of Mexico.

Campa and Goldberg (2005).

Calderon C. and K. Schmidt-Hebbel (2008), Business Cycles and Fiscal Policies: the Role of Institutions and financial Markets, Working paper No. 481 Central Bank of Chile, Santiago.

Haber, S. (2006), Why banks Don't Lend: The Mexican financial System, Stanford University.

IMF (2007), Mexico: Financial Sector Assessment Program Update—Technical Note—Risk Management Practices and Stress Tests of Commercial Banks, The Insurance Sector, and the Derivatives Exchange , Country Report No. 07/165.

IMF (2009a), Mexico: Selected Issues, IMF Country Report No. 09/54.

IMF (2009b), Mexico: Arrangement Under the Flexible Credit Line – Staff Report; Staff Supplement; and Press Release on the Executive Board Discussion, Country Report No. 09/126.

IMF (2009c), IMF note on global economic policies and prospects prepared for the March 13-14, 2009 meeting in London of the Group of Twenty Ministers and Central Bank Governors.

Harding, D. and A. Pagan (2002), "Dissecting the cycle: a methodological investigation", *Journal of Monetary Economics* 49: 365-381.

OECD, 2009, Going for Growth, Paris, OECD.

Perry G. *et al.* (2008), Fiscal policy, stabilization, and growth: prudence or abstinence?, edited by Guillermo E. Perry, Luis Serven, and Rodrigo Suescun, World Bank.

Pew Hispanic Center (2009), Mexican Immigrants in the United States in 2008.

INS (2008), Sistema de Protección Social en Salud. Evaluación de Procesos Administrativos, Instituto Nacional de Salud Pública.

Ramos-Francia, M. and A. Torres Garcia (2006), "Inflation dynamics in Mexico: A characterization using the New Phillips Curve", Banco de México Working Papers No. 2006-15.

Schmidt-Hebbel, K. and A. Werner (2002), "Inflation targeting in Brazil, Chile and Mexico: Performance, credibility and the exchange rate", *Economía* 2(2): 31-89.

Schultz, P. (2004), "School subsidies for the poor: evaluating the Mexican Progresa poverty program", *Journal of Development Economics* 74: 199-250.

Sidaoui, J. and M. Ramos Francia (2008), The monetary transmission mechanism in Mexico: recent developments, in *Transmission mechanisms for monetary policy in emerging market economies*, 2008, vol. 35, pp 363-394, *Bank for International Settlements*.

Todd, P. and K. Wolpin (2006), "Assessing the impact of a school subsidy programme in Mexico: Using a social experiment to validate a dynamic behavioural model of child schooling and fertility", *American Economic Review* 96: 1384-1417.

ISBN 978-92-64-05441-7
OECD Economic Surveys: Mexico
© OECD 2009

Chapter 2

Managing the oil economy – Can Mexico do it better?

Fiscal policy is highly dependent on volatile oil income. The balanced budget rule can create a bias for spending oil revenues as they are earned, especially as transfers to the stabilization funds are limited by caps at low levels. This can potentially lead to a pro-cyclical bias in fiscal policy. Revenues have also been lower than they could have, if gasoline prices had adjusted with international prices instead of a price smoothing mechanism for the domestic price. The system also benefits mostly well-off consumers and has important environmental costs. To better manage budget cycles and oil wealth, Mexico should establish a structural deficit fiscal rule. To improve transparency oil revenues should be reported in gross terms in the budget. A price mechanism that leads to a closer alignment between domestic and international gasoline prices should be adopted and other energy subsidies eliminated and an energy excise tax introduced. To reduce dependence on oil revenues and prepare for the exhaustion of oil reserves, further tax reform is needed to cut exemptions and broaden the tax base. A rapid and adequate implementation of the reform of the state oil company is required to boost oil revenues, increase efficiency and investment in future exploration. While the recent reform passed by congress is expected to improve governance and allow Pemex to use performance based contracts, its implementation is key.

Mexico's challenges with oil revenues

Responsible handling of revenue from natural resources can be a source of wealth, economic growth and stability for a country. However, the volatility, uncertainty and exhaustibility of these revenues, and the fact that they largely originate from abroad, is a challenge to policy. Many oil producing countries have found it difficult to smooth government expenditure over time and decouple it from the short-term volatility of oil revenues leading to occasional boom-bust cycles. Thus in practice many countries have found oil to be more of a curse than a blessing. Despite the oil wealth, many oil-producing countries have a poor growth record (Gelb 1988, Fatas and Mihov 2003).

Resource-rich emerging economies are increasingly using fiscal rules to help manage public finances (Box 2.1). Properly designed rules can have large benefits in terms of

---

Box 2.1. **Mexico, Chile and Norway:**
Different ways to deal with resource revenues

Norway – The Government Pension Fund.

Oil and gas exports were over 20% of GDP in 2007 with a substantial impact on public finances. All revenues from the petroleum sector are channeled directly into the Government Pension Fund to isolate the government's budget from the volatility of oil prices and to save oil wealth for future generations, including providing for growing pension liabilities. The funds are invested abroad with the Ministry of Finance setting the guidelines, and the central bank doing the active management of the resources. Proceeds from the fund finance the non-oil structural budget deficit. This deficit is set at a level of expected long run real returns (4%) from the fund, which in recent years has corresponded to about 4-5% of GDP. The rule allows for active demand management in that the non-oil structural deficit target can be breached for countercyclical purposes. The assets of the Fund at end-2008 were about 125% of non-oil GDP, or 90% of total GDP.

The fiscal rule has had a positive impact on the economy and public finances. It has avoided a potentially destabilizing impact of highly variable export revenues on the exchange rate and demand on the mainland economy. As the fund holds its assets overseas, the currency flows generated from the offshore sector are automatically neutralized. However, the fund has been criticized for providing too much stimulus to the economy, as the 4% return is likely to increase over time along with the value of the assets, and that the savings generated are not sufficient to meet future pension liabilities (OECD 2008).

Chile – The Copper Stabilization Fund

The copper sector is a dominant part of the Chilean economy with about 50% of exports and 8% of GDP. Public sector revenues from copper have varied between 5-17% of total tax collection. The sector consists of a state-owned Codelco, and a number of private operators with about 30-70% of output respectively.

Box 2.1. **Mexico, Chile and Norway:** Different ways to deal with resource revenues *(cont.)*

A fiscal rule was established to smooth fluctuations in copper revenues and related spending in the budget. Chile has a fiscal rule that defines a structural surplus at a certain level, which in recent years has been 0.5% to 1% of GDP. The surplus target was set so that enough savings can be accumulated to finance future public commitments, in particular a guaranteed minimum pension and old-age benefit, and recapitalization of the central bank. The surplus target is made of a non-oil structural surplus and estimated long-term copper revenues based on a reference price. When copper prices exceed/are below a reference price, that is assumed to reflect a medium-term equilibrium price for copper, revenues are transferred to and from the copper fund. The Government is also authorized to transfer 10% of CODELCO-sales to military procurement.

The reference price and the potential output used for the deficit rule are estimated by independent expert panels. The members represent academia, the financial and the mining sector. For copper, the experts submit their reference price projections for the next 10 years, which is then averaged to get the reference price for the budget each year. The resulting prices have been conservative in view of the commodity boom of recent years, resulting in large savings of about 12% of GDP at end 2008 even after paying off public debt.

These rules have enhanced transparency and discipline in fiscal policy. As automatic stabilizers are small, the fund has enabled Chile to conduct counter cyclical fiscal policy in downturns, when access to foreign credit has become more expensive, as in the current crisis. The fund has been successful in reducing output volatility (Larrain-Parro 2008, Fiess 2002, Rodriquez *et al.* 2007), and has made Chile one of the few emerging markets able to conduct strong counter-cyclical fiscal policies (Perry *et al.* 2008).

Mexico – The Oil Stabilization Funds

Oil accounts for about 5-6% of GDP, 10-15% of exports and 30-40% of fiscal revenues. The sector is dominated by state-owned Pemex, which is responsible for production, distribution and imports of oil and gas products. The central bank buys all foreign exchange from Pemex, and limits the currency inflow to the economy to reduce pressures on the exchange rate from oil revenues (OECD 2007).

Three Mexican oil revenue stabilization funds – for the Federal Government, PEMEX and State Governments – the first was established in 2000 and the other two in 2006 to reduce oil-related volatility in the budget. This reflected the desire to avoid unplanned budget cuts if prices declined, as was the case in the aftermath of the Tequila crisis in the mid 1990's. The rules of the funds were refined in the 2006 Fiscal Responsibility Law, and again in the 2009 budget. The Law also included provisions for setting a reference price for oil and transfers to the funds. The Federal Government fund is managed by the Ministry of Finance, and has a target level for savings, which was 56 billion pesos (0.5% of GDP) in 2008. The law envisages that 40% of excess revenues are allocated to the Federal Government fund, and 25% to the PEMEX and State Government funds each, for total savings of 90%, with the remaining 10% being transferred to states for investment. Once the funds have reached their limit, 75% of excess revenues are allocated to investment, and 25% to a Fund to Support the Restructuring of Pension Systems. The target savings level was almost doubled in the budget for 2009. Before transferring excess revenues to the funds, however, some items are deducted (shortfalls inrevenues with respect to the budget, changes in energy costs that are not fully reflected in domestic electricity tariffs, costs of natural disasters and outlays resulting from changes in non-programmable expenditures due to changes in interest or exchange rates). At end-2008 the funds' cumulative reserves were 145 billion pesos or 1.2% of GDP.

> ### Box 2.1. **Mexico, Chile and Norway:**
> ### **Different ways to deal with resource revenues** (cont.)
>
> In contrast to Chile and Norway, the Mexican funds have accumulated limited savings due to the caps on their size. While all government oil revenues in Norway and excess revenues in Chile are channeled into the funds, the net accumulation in Mexico has been much smaller. Although excess revenues have been potentially large, low caps on the accumulated savings in the funds have led to a significant proportion of the excess revenues being spent on investment projects.

reduced volatility, inter-generational equity, building buffers for bad times, policy credibility, and sustainability of priority expenditures. (Kopitz *et al*. 2004). The rules should be transparent, make economic sense in view of a country's circumstances, and simple to understand and monitor. It is also important to make the breach of fiscal rules costly. The rules can be particularly useful in allocating spending in countries that may be subject to political bias.

Mexico is facing many fiscal policy challenges from its oil wealth, and has adopted fiscal rules to help in its management. However, the current rules – the balanced budget rule, excess revenues allocation rules and capped savings in the stabilisation funds – do not mitigate volatility of spending and revenues as much as might be desired. In addition, revenues have been smaller than they could have been due to the existence of inefficient energy subsidies and a price smoothing mechanism for gasoline prices. Longer term fiscal sustainability is also a concern as the budget relies heavily on oil revenues, which are set to decline in the future. Even though past underinvestment by the oil company has been reversed since 2005, an expedite and adequate implementation of the energy sector reform approved in 2008 is necessary to promote additional increase in investment as well as technology transfers. In the near term, Mexico needs to deal with these challenges – volatility, efficient use of oil revenues over time, and preparing for a time period after oil resources are depleted. Building on previous *Surveys* (OECD 2007), this chapter discusses how Mexico can deal with these challenges.

Dealing with volatility

The current fiscal framework has led to limited smoothing of the impact of revenue volatility on public expenditures. The volatility of public consumption and GDP in Mexico are high compared to other OECD emerging markets (Figure 2.1), and expenditure to GDP ratios have moved along with revenues. (Figure 2.2). Volatility can have high costs. It tends to be negatively correlated with investment ratios, can lead to short-term bias in fiscal policy, and destroy human and physical capital during deep recessions, so strengthening the mechanisms in the budget to limit expenditure volatility is desirable. Poverty and education outlays can also be adversely affected (Serven 2007). Volatility can be smoothed by a more gradual injection of oil revenues to the economy, particularly by increasing the caps on the stabilization funds. This would have the additional benefit of counting with a larger fiscal cushion in economic downturns, as debt-financing of larger deficits can be costly amid a general rise in perceptions of risks. Reforming the fiscal rules to reduce volatility is thus an important challenge.

Figure 2.1. **Volatility of GDP and public consumption**[1]

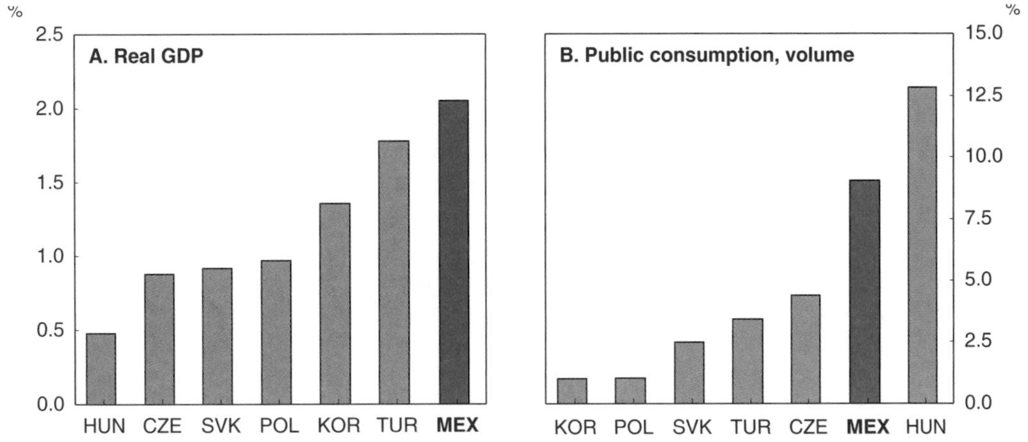

1. Measured by the coefficient of variation of real GDP and public consumption during 1995 Q1-2008 Q2 period.
Source: OECD, National Accounts.

StatLink 🔗 http://dx.doi.org/10.1787/683877642883

Figure 2.2. **Mexico: Revenues and expenditure** [1]
As a share of GDP

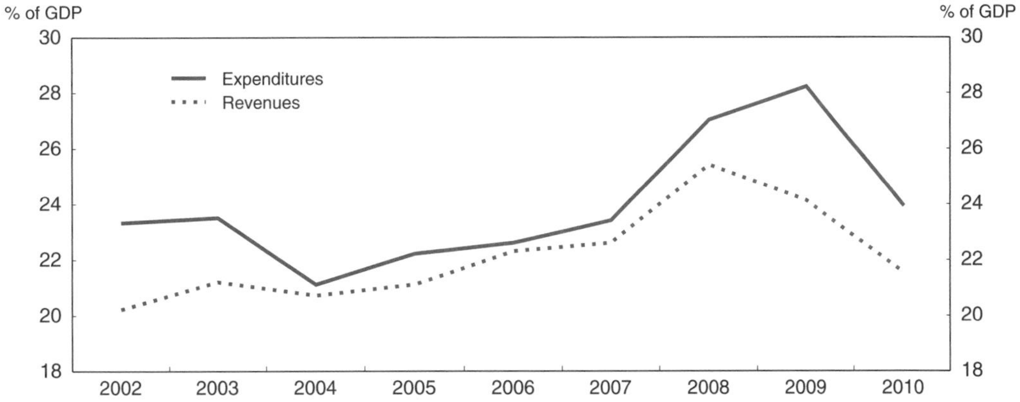

1. Includes the traditional budget and financing operations. Gasoline subsidies recorded as spending and oil revenues in gross terms. LP and electricity subsidies not included.
Source: SHCP.

StatLink 🔗 http://dx.doi.org/10.1787/684024020585

Mexican fiscal rules

A basic pillar of Mexico's fiscal policy is the balanced budget rule, aimed at ensuring fiscal sustainability. The rule applies to the "traditional budget" part of Mexican fiscal deficit, as lending operations are outside its scope (see Chapter 1). It has been successful in establishing fiscal discipline and reducing gross public debt to about 40% of GDP after it had ballooned following the Tequila crisis in the mid-1990's. On the other hand, the rule has a pro-cyclical bias from one budget exercise to the next as larger tax revenues tend to be spent at the time they are collected. From the point of view of oil revenues, it might also be possible to improve on the formula that is used to approximate for the "structural" level of oil prices.

Mexico has tried to smooth revenue volatility by establishing stabilization funds. In principle, oil revenues that exceed the annually set reference price are transferred to the

Box 2.2. **Oil price projections in the budget**

Until recently oil price forecasts used in Mexican budgets over the years have been conservative compared either to those obtained by other methods (moving average, long term trend (HP filter) or actual prices (Figure 2.3). While conservative price setting is a prudent fiscal practice, it is important that it is complemented with large limits in the oil stabilization funds to make sure that a larger amount of resources are available when needed. Since 2000 actual oil prices have been substantially higher than those projected in the budget (Figure 2.3). While it is difficult to project oil prices given the large volatilities in world oil prices in recent years, this underlines the importance of transparent and clear rules for using excess revenues in the budget.

Figure 2.3. **Simulations of oil price forecasts in Mexico and actual prices**

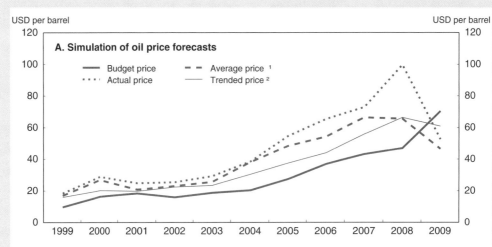

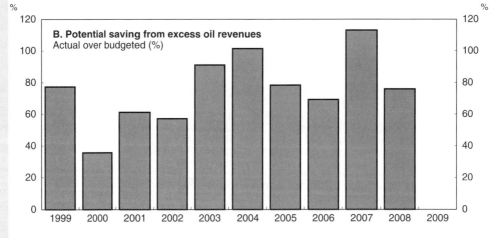

1. Moving average of the last three years and one-year-ahead futures price.
2. Using a Hodrick-Prescot filter.

Source: OECD, SHCP.

StatLink http://dx.doi.org/10.1787/684108613501

funds. However, despite the quadrupling of oil prices in recent years the funds have accumulated low savings – the balance at end 2008 stood at 1.2% of GDP (Box 2.1). This reflects both the low accumulation limits set to the funds-about 1.2% of GDP or 145 billion pesos in 2008-, the use of excess revenues to additional investments that are carried out once the funds have reached their limits, and the deductions from these revenues to compensate for revenue shortcomings from other sources, and electricity price support. As a result, volatility of spending has remained.

Before the current framework was in place, setting the reference price had been a complex process reflecting the difficulty of forecasting future oil prices. Until 2006 the price was negotiated and tended to remain consistently well below actual prices in a context of increasing international prices. Formulas based on moving averages or model predictions, which are used by a number of other oil producers, would have resulted in higher prices, even though it is clear that these are affected by the rising trend that was observed *ex post* (Box 2.2). The 2006 Fiscal Responsibility Law introduced a formula for the reference price, basing it on a weighted average of past and future medium-term price trends and short-term futures prices. The functioning of the new formula is still being tested, but the equal weight given to the short term trends tends to bias the reference price towards the prevailing market price (upwards until recently).[1] For example, in 2009 the formula produced a price of USD 70 (it was set before the collapse of prices in late 2008).

A reform to the fiscal rule approved in 2008 exempts Pemex investment spending from the balanced budget provision. While these investments have always been part of the broader fiscal deficit, until 2008 most of them were recorded in lending operations. As of 2009 the investment outlays were included in the "traditional budget" part of the deficit, but outside the balanced budget rule. This budgetary practice has contributed to revenue and spending volatility under the balanced budget rule, as Pemex revenues tend to move with oil prices, while its current spending is more stable. Thus, for example, in 2006 and 2007 the net impact of Pemex in the traditional budget was about 1.5% of GDP, which enabled correspondingly higher spending under the balanced budget rule (Figure 2.4 and Table 2.1).While this may have enabled financing higher social spending in boom years, a severe downturn in oil prices can rapidly lead to financing problems and cuts in programs.

Figure 2.4. **Oil revenues in the budget**

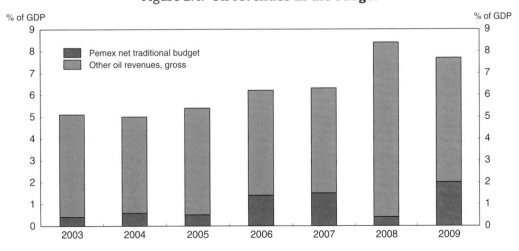

Source: Ministry of Finance and PEMEX.

StatLink ⟍⟍⟍ http://dx.doi.org/10.1787/684136705275

Table 2.1. **Mexico: Oil-related fiscal indicators (per cent of GDP)**

	2003	2004	2005	2006	2007	2008
Budget	–0.6	–0.2	–0.1	0.1	0.0	0.0
Fiscal balance (budget + net lending)	–2.4	–0.4	–1.1	–0.3	–0.7	–1.0
Oil related indicators						
Pemex revenues	2.3	2.2	2.0	3.1	3.3	3.0
Pemex current spending	2.0	2.0	2.0	2.1	1.9	2.1
Pemex net budget	0.4	0.6	0.5	1.4	1.5	0.4
Pemex net (incl. inv.)	–0.5	–0.3	–0.2	0.5	0.6	–0.1
Other oil revenues	4.7	4.4	4.9	4.8	4.7	7.7
Oil total	7.1	6.7	6.9	7.9	8.1	10.7
Tax/price support on oil consumption (IEPS)	1.2	0.6	0.2	–0.4	–0.4	–1.8
Budget less Pemex	–1.1	–0.6	–0.3	0.6	0.7	–0.1
Fiscal balance less Pemex	–1.9	–0.1	–0.8	–0.8	–1.4	–1.0
Revenues*	21.2	20.7	21.1	22.3	22.6	25.4
non-oil	14.1	13.6	13.7	14.0	14.4	14.7
oil	7.1	6.7	6.9	7.9	8.1	10.7
Expenditure	23.5	21.1	22.2	22.6	23.4	26.5
Non-oil balance	–9.5	–8.0	–8.7	–8.7	–8.9	–10.9
Underlying non-oil balance	–6.8	–6.1	–5.9	–6.1	–7.3	–9.2
Underlying balance	–3.3	–2.1	–0.8	–0.8	–1.4	–3.2

* reported with gross oil revenues with the oil price support as part of expenditures (budget+net lending). Costs of LP and electricity subsidies not included.
Source: SHCP, OECD estimates.

Reforming the fiscal rules

To smooth the injection of revenues into the economy Mexico should introduce a structural deficit rule that sets a limit for the cyclically adjusted non-oil fiscal deficit. This would smooth spending in line with growth, lead to automatic savings when oil revenues are high and the economic cycle is up, and automatic spending when the oil and non-oil revenues are low. Oil revenues would thus go to a fund that would gradually inject oil wealth into the economy and help to stabilize future short-falls. The structural non-oil balance would also facilitate assessment of the fiscal policy stance in the economy. By excluding oil revenues (mostly from abroad) and oil production associated expenditures, and other cyclically sensitive items, emphasis on a non-oil fiscal deficit would enable a clearer measurement of the government's discretionary fiscal decisions on domestic demand.

The level of the deficit could be linked to a certain level of net assets to GDP either in current or present value terms, or to structural measurements of income. However, the calculation of net assets and of structural income raises a number of challenges. In terms of net assets, present values require estimating the value of future streams of oil revenues, discount rates and the value of other government assets and liabilities. Structural income calculations require assessments of the elasticities of revenues to income and of the output gap. To ensure transparency and avoid political biases, these parameters could be estimated by an independent panel and monitored regularly, so as to keep the net financial position of the government stable. As oil wealth in Mexico is set to decline in the future this would require a gradual lowering of public debt over time and/or an increase in non-oil revenues to keep the structural deficit at a certain level. To avoid complications created by Pemex in the calculation of the non-oil structural deficit, it would need to be taken out of this measurement of the fiscal balance. Nevertheless, given the importance of Pemex it is still important that full information is provided on the company and on the fiscal implications of its budget.

The impact on volatility of a rule base on net wealth would depend on how the relationship between the size of the deficit and net wealth is defined. As net assets, whether at current or present values, can be volatile especially with oil, the deficit target should be set for a number of years and adjusted only infrequently as in Norway or Chile. One could also look at the government's net assets over the past cycle (oil revenues, debt etc.). Another source of potential volatility for the target is the denominator, GDP. To avoid this, the literature generally recommends using non-oil GDP (Medas-Sakharova 2009). Mexico should consider this as well, although its non-oil GDP has been relatively steady at about 95% of GDP making this adjustment less important. As discussed later, the relationship between the deficit and a structural estimation is more straightforward.

Another option is to define a cyclically adjusted deficit as a sum of an estimate of a structural (permanent) component of oil revenues, in addition to the non-oil structural deficit. This is the method used by Chile (Box 2.1), and is similar to what the Mexican formula for the determination of oil prices tries to do. The size of the deficit can be set so that, for example, public debt would remain constant at a certain level. As this option requires estimating the reference price for oil in the budget, a review of the results that have been obtained with the formula that Mexican authorities use for determining the budget price is relevant. Oil revenues above the reference price would be transferred to a fund, which would be drawn upon when revenues fall below the reference price or when there is a need for discretionary fiscal stimulus in a downturn. Either method would require some estimates of future oil prices. This is complicated by the fact that prices of oil and many other commodities tend to be non-stationary – without a clear equilibrium level.[2] Rules based on non-stationary moving averages etc. can lead to continued accumulation/decumulation of revenues, instead of some smoothing over cycles. The reference price can also become a target of political influence. To ensure neutrality, expert panels estimate both the reference price and potential output in Chile, which are the basis for the structural balance calculations in the budget. Mexico uses a formula with both backward and forward looking components. Colombia, Ecuador, Nigeria, and Venezuela use reference prices based on moving averages. The attractiveness of either option would largely depend on the difficulty of estimating either the net asset position or the medium-term reference oil price.

To increase transparency in the use of oil revenues, the fiscal tables should report oil income on a gross basis (Box 2.3), and the various adjustments to the oil price before transfers to the stabilization funds should be eliminated and included as spending in a normal budget process.

Spending of oil revenues-efficiency and timing

Countries with exhaustible natural resources need also to decide how to share the revenues between generations. An important factor in determining whether spending today versus in the future is desirable is the state of development of a country or the nature of public assets and liabilities. Emerging countries may want to favour current spending as investing in education or infrastructure can have high pay-offs in terms of future growth. More mature economies may be better off in saving, for example, for increasing future pension liabilities.

Box 2.3. **Mexico – Accounting issues with oil revenues**

Assessing the role of oil in the budget requires some adjustments to both revenues and spending as oil revenues are currently reported on a net basis. Despite the increase in oil prices from about USD 30 to USD 140 per barrel between 2006 and 2008 (or from USD 53 to USD 84 in annual averages) reported oil revenues in the budget have been relatively stable and increased only slightly. Although this is partly due to declining production volumes– oil production is down by about 20 per cent from its peak in 2006 – and an appreciation of the real exchange rate during the period, it also reflects the foregone revenues associated with the gasoline price smoothing mechanism as domestic prices deviated from their international references, with gasoline imports being paid at international prices. To better understand the sources and uses of income and macroeconomic effects of the oil economy, oil revenues should be recorded in gross terms and energy price support as expenditure. This could also reveal a higher volatility of oil revenues than reported in the budget numbers in recent years.

In Mexico it seems both efficient and fair that the current generation spends part of the revenues to finance development. Therefore, there is a delicate balance between saving for smoothing the injection of the revenues over time and having a cushion for counter-cyclical fiscal policy, and using part of the resources for development. Mexico's social investment needs are substantial in education and health (Chapter 3). Similarly, growth-boosting public investments are needed in infrastructure (Chapter 4). However, for these growth dividends to materialize it is important to spend the money in an efficient way on high quality projects.

While the oil wealth has helped finance many important investments in Mexico, it is important to improve the efficiency of spending. One example is the gasoline price smoothing mechanism and energy subsidies (see Box 2.1). Gasoline prices are kept stable in real terms which led to foregone income from 2006 to 2008 as the international price increased (Table 2.2). When world oil prices are above USD 40-45 per barrel (at current exchange rates) the Mexican price mechanism requires a subsidy, while there is a tax when prices are below this level. LP gas and electricity prices faced by households benefit from straight subsidies. The cost of the former is borne by Pemex in lower revenues, and the latter is financed by the state electricity company. In 2008 these three types of subsidies cost the budget about 2.7% of GDP, in addition to potential lost excise revenue (Table 2.3).

While keeping energy prices stable may have stabilized energy demand and helped contain inflation during the recent commodity boom, this policy has led to inefficient and unequal spending in a country with substantial social challenges. For example, the cost of the regressive energy subsidies and gasoline price smoothing mechanism in 2008 was more than twice the amount spent on anti-poverty programmes and 1.4 times the health budget. Most of the subsidy is captured by the better-off that tend to buy most gasoline and

Table 2.2. **Mexico: Gasoline prices in international comparison (pesos per liter)**

	2005	2006	2007	2008	2009 (Jan-Feb)
Mexico (regular)	6.3	6.6	6.9	7.3	7.7
US (regular)	6.4	7.3	8.0	9.3	7.0
France (premium)	19.0	17.4	18.7	21.8	22.5

Source: SHCP, Pemex, Eurostat.

Table 2.3. **Energy subsidies in Mexico (% of GDP)**

	2002	2004	2005	2006	2007	2008
LP gas	0.0	0.1	0.1	0.0	0.1	0.2
Electricity	0.6	0.6	0.7	0.6	0.6	0.7
Gasoline (IEPS)	–1.2	–0.6	–0.2	0.4	0.4	1.8
Total	–0.6	0.1	0.5	1.1	1.2	2.7

Source: SHCP.

electricity (Chapter 1). The policy also distorts resource allocation by reducing incentives for energy saving investment, and contributes to congestion and burning of hydrocarbons, with detrimental effects on greenhouse gas emission and climate change.

To increase the efficiency of spending, the stabilization scheme for the gasoline price should be replaced with a mechanism that aligns domestic with international prices together with an excise tax, and other energy subsidies removed. Although the price stabilization scheme turns to a tax when prices are low (as in early 2009), it would be more efficient to let prices move in line with market prices and impose an excise tax on gasoline.[3] This would better deal with environmental costs, promote a sustainable use of energy resources and bring additional revenues for the government. There is a strong likelihood for the need for more subsidies under the current scheme as world oil prices recover. More vulnerable groups can be better protected from higher energy costs by targeted income support. During the transition period any gasoline price support should be reported as part of expenditure instead of a negative tax in the current budget, and the other energy subsidies reported explicitly as expenditure.

Preparing for a world with less oil resources

Tax reform is also needed to reduce dependence on declining oil revenues

The budget relies heavily on volatile and uncertain oil income – 30-40% of total budget revenues – that are set to decline with the shrinking oil production. Even though the recently approved fiscal reform increased non-oil tax revenues, these are still low by any standard at about 10% of GDP, reflecting a plethora of exemptions. The large size of the informal sector, which many observers estimate at 25-40% (EIU 2008, IMF 2007), also reduces the tax base. Efforts at reforming the tax system have been difficult, as the abundance of oil income, especially in recent years, has reduced political incentives for increasing other taxes. The narrow tax base and the volatility of oil revenues are a risk for future fiscal sustainability when oil prices and production are declining and can make it difficult to sustain funding for important social programmes.

The authorities initiated a tax reform in 2007 to gradually broaden the base for non-oil taxes (see OECD 2007) and make the economy less dependent on oil revenues. The measures also aimed at improving tax collection and reducing exemptions. One important step was the introduction of an alternative minimum income tax (IETU) aimed at bringing smaller enterprises to the tax net from the informal sector. To increase incentives for reporting and to capture resources from the informal sector of the economy, the package included a tax-deductible contribution on monthly deposits made in cash above a certain minimum amount. Deposits through other means such as checks or electronic transfers are not subject to the contribution, and by being tax-deductible the contribution on cash deposits does not affect formal businesses that are reporting adequately. More time is required to evaluate the full effects of the reform. The IETU tax collection in 2008 was only about two thirds of the target, though some of this might have been due to the slowdown in activity, and the fact that some of the collection from the tax was reflected in higher income tax revenues.[4] The government is well aware of the need for further tax reform to replace declining oil revenues over time, and it should undertake action as early as when the budget for next year is submitted to Congress in September 2009. The announcement of no tax cuts in the January 2009 stimulus package is welcome.

The recommendations in the 2007 *Survey of Mexico* on further tax reform remain valid. This should include measures to curtail exemptions that currently erode the tax base, in particular on direct taxes in terms of various preferential regimes and tax deductions. The tax base can also be increased by broadening the VAT tax, for example by reducing zero-rating of certain items. The collection threshold can also be increased to enhance compliance and tax control.

An expedite and adequate implementation of the reform of Pemex is needed to improve the efficiency of the oil economy and maximize oil income. Additional reform should be considered if necessary

Pemex is an important but declining part of the Mexican economy. It accounts for about 5% of GDP and 15% of exports. Mexico is also an important player in the world oil economy—it is the 6th largest producer with 5% of world gas and petroleum output in 2006. However, the sector is shrinking as production and proven reserves are declining. As a consequence of higher domestic demand, oil exports have dropped even faster and imports of refined products increased. PEMEX estimates that there are only 8-9 years of oil reserves left in the currently operated oil fields at today's production levels. Geological surveys point to potentially large, untapped reserves extending production for another 9-10 years, but their assessment would require substantial investments. An equal amount of reserves are estimated to lie in deep waters, which Mexico, previously to the Pemex reform, was unable to access for lack of funds, technology or expertise.

To revamp the oil sector, an adequate implementation of the Pemex reform is urgently needed. Pemex is state owned by constitution and beset with political interference and strong unions that have resisted reform in the past (Walton and Guerrero 2006). The decline in production and proven reserves reflects low efficiency, weak governance, and underinvestment in both up- and downstream and maintenance and insufficient refining capacity. As a result Mexico may soon become a net importer of oil (IMF 2009)-oil imports already account for about three quarters of oil exports. Much of this reflects politicization of management decisions (Pemex is part of the federal budget) and reliance on the government with many competing objectives for financing its investment needs. If adequately implemented, the approved reform should contribute to the resolution of these problems as it aims at strengthening corporate governance and it excluded Pemex's investment from the balanced budget rule.

In October 2008 the Mexican Congress passed a highly overdue reform for the petroleum sector addressing some of these issues. The main elements of the reform relate to improving governance, as well as allowing for the establishment of performance based contracts. Both the Director and the Board were given increased control over funds and investment decisions that previously required congressional approval. The Board also has the option to use some of the revenue surplus, approve changes to the PEMEX-budget and decide on the operational use of resources, without congressional approval. This could be important, as strategic decisions often have to be taken quickly, as petroleum search and extraction equipment are scarce, and in high demand. The appointment of four independent Board members in addition to the current 11, who are mainly representatives from the Government and the union, should reduce political influence. PEMEX financing possibilities and corporate governance will be improved through the issuance of citizen bonds. Although its high existing debt may limit borrowing, introduction of the bonds can make a precedent for taking on board the concern for returns by investors. The reform also introduces more flexibility for contracting, including the possibility to use performance bonuses for subcontractors which could potentially lead to a significant increase of investment in the sector.

The reform might nevertheless not be enough to reverse the decline in production, and results will not be observed immediately. The strict exclusion of all foreign ownership of oil reserves or any other basic petrochemical activities by the constitution implies that equity joint ventures between Mexico and other oil companies, including with other nationalized companies, are explicitly excluded. This makes Mexico's petroleum sector a relatively closed one. It will also need creative solutions on how to attract funds with various incentive schemes not to breach the constitution.

Concluding remarks

Mexico has been successful in improving fiscal sustainability, but it could do better in managing its oil wealth. Volatility of revenues from one budget exercise to the next, as oil cycles tend to coincide with business cycles, and more efficient use of oil revenue gains remain important challenges. In addition, Mexico has to get ready for lower oil revenues as production is in rapid decline. To deal with these challenges, Mexico should introduce a structural non-oil deficit fiscal rule based on keeping net wealth at a certain level relative to net public assets or based on structural measures of both oil and non-oil income. Scrapping the inefficient and regressive energy subsidies and adopting a mechanism for

---

Box 2.4. **Key recommendations**

Adjust the fiscal framework to reduce the pro-cyclicality of the fiscal balance and make better use of oil revenue

- Replace the nominal balanced budget rule by a limit on the non-oil structural deficit, so as to improve short-run stabilisation policies and smooth the injection of oil wealth into the economy.

- Regularly review the limit for the non-oil structural deficit, so as to stabilize the net financial position of the public sector.

- Report energy subsidies and price smoothing opportunity cost as expenditure (not as a negative tax currently).

- Establish a mechanism that guarantees that gasoline prices do not deviate from their international reference, which can be easier now when prices are low. Replace the IEPS (stabilization tax/subsidy) with an excise tax.

- Continue tax reform to make the budget less dependent on oil revenues by enlarging the base (see 2007 Survey for more details).

- Implement and continue PEMEX-reform to improve incentives for private sector participation in exploration, transport and refining.

---

the determination of gasoline prices that ensures that no large deviations arise between domestic and international prices would release revenues for social and infrastructure investments with large future pay-offs. The non-oil tax base should be broadened, and the reform of Pemex should be implemented as quickly as possible, and if need be deepened, to increase exploration and improve efficiency of the company.

Notes

1. The formula gives 25% weights to the average price for past 10 years, 25% to the average futures price for the next 3 years and 50% for the futures prices of the next few months adjusted by a factor of 0.86. In the 2009 budget the calculation resulted in USD 36, USD 105 and USD 90 for the three components with an average price of USD 70.

2. Unit root tests on both oil and copper confirm non-stationarity.

3. The IEPS (gasoline tax/subsidy) used to yield revenues of 1-2% of GDP in the early 2000's but in recent years the maintenance of the gasoline price well below world prices has resulted in subsidies or low tax incidence.

4. The IETU is a minimum tax associated with the corporate income tax. Therefore, some firms which were required to pay IETU might have decided to pay a higher income tax to consolidate with parent companies abroad.

Bibliography

EIU (2008), Country Profile Mexico, London.

Fatas, A. and I. Mihov (2003). "The Case For Restricting Fiscal Policy Discretion,"The Quarterly Journal of Economics, MIT Press, Vol. 118(4), pages 1419-1447, November.

Fiess, N. (2002), Chile new fiscal rule, Office of the chief economist, World Bank.

Gelb, A. (1988), Oil Windfalls: Blessing or Curse? New York; Oxford University Press.

IMF (2007), Article IV consultation for Mexico 2007, Staff Report, Country Report No. 07/379.

IMF (2009), Article IV Consultation for Mexico 2009, Staff Report, Country Report No. 09/53.

Kopitz et al. (2004), Rules-Based Fiscal Policy in Emerging Markets. Background, Analysis and Prospects, Edited by George Kopits, Palgrave Macmillan.

Larrain, P and F. Parro (2008), Chile menos volatile, El trimestre economico, Vol. LXXV (3), No. 299, Julio-septiembre de 2008, pp. 563-596.

Medas P. and D. Sakharova (2009), A Primer on Fiscal Analysis in Oil-Producing Countries, IMF Working Paper No. 09/56.

OECD (2007), OECD Survey of Mexico, Paris.

OECD (2008), OECD Survey of Norway, Paris.

Perry G. (2008), Fiscal policy, stabilization, and growth: prudence or abstinence? edited by Guillermo E. Perry, Luis Serven, and Rodrigo Suescun, World Bank.

Rodríguez, J., C. Tokman and A. Vega (2007), Structural balance policy in Chile, OECD, Journal of Budgeting, Vol. 7(2), pp. 59-92.

Serven L. (2007), "Fiscal rules, public investment, and growth," Policy Research Working Paper Series 4382, World Bank.

Walton M., I.Guerrero and Lopez Calva (2006), "The Inequality Trap and its Links to Low Growth in Mexico". Paper presented at World Bank-Harvard Rockefeller Center conference on equity and growth in Mexico, Mexico City November 27-28th, 2006.

ISBN 978-92-64-05441-7
OECD Economic Surveys: Mexico
© OECD 2009

Chapter 3

Achieving higher performance: Enhancing spending efficiency in health and education

Despite progress over the past two decades Mexico's health and education indicators remain well below the average of the OECD and some of its Latin American emerging market peers. Health insurance coverage is incomplete, especially for low-income families, and access to health services is highly uneven. There are several separate vertically integrated insurance networks, which increases administrative costs and results in an inefficient use of facilities. In education, lower secondary schools enroll only two thirds of the relevant age group and the quality of education is low, as indicated by poor PISA scores. This reflects poor teaching quality, a consequence of non-transparent teacher selection processes until recently, and limited school autonomy in budgeting, instruction and personnel decisions. Accountability to the government and parents is also low as there is no national exit exam after secondary education and the existing evaluation schemes are fragmented. Recent health and education reforms have started to address these issues, but more needs to be done to increase the efficiency of spending by increasing the coverage of health insurance, reducing the fragmentation of the health system, increasing enrolment in lower secondary education, and improving the quality of teaching.

Introduction

Mexico's health and education indicators lag behind those of higher income OECD countries and of some Latin American emerging markets. Although population health indicators have improved over the past two decades, life expectancy at birth remains lower and child mortality higher than in most OECD countries. Mexico also ranks at the bottom of the OECD in secondary school enrolment and on standardised student tests. This partly reflects Mexico's level of per capita income and per capita spending on health and education. Compared to other emerging markets with similar spending levels, Mexico performs about average but better outcomes in some Latin American countries suggest that there is scope for improving the efficiency of spending (Figure 3.1).

Figure 3.1. **Performance in health and education**

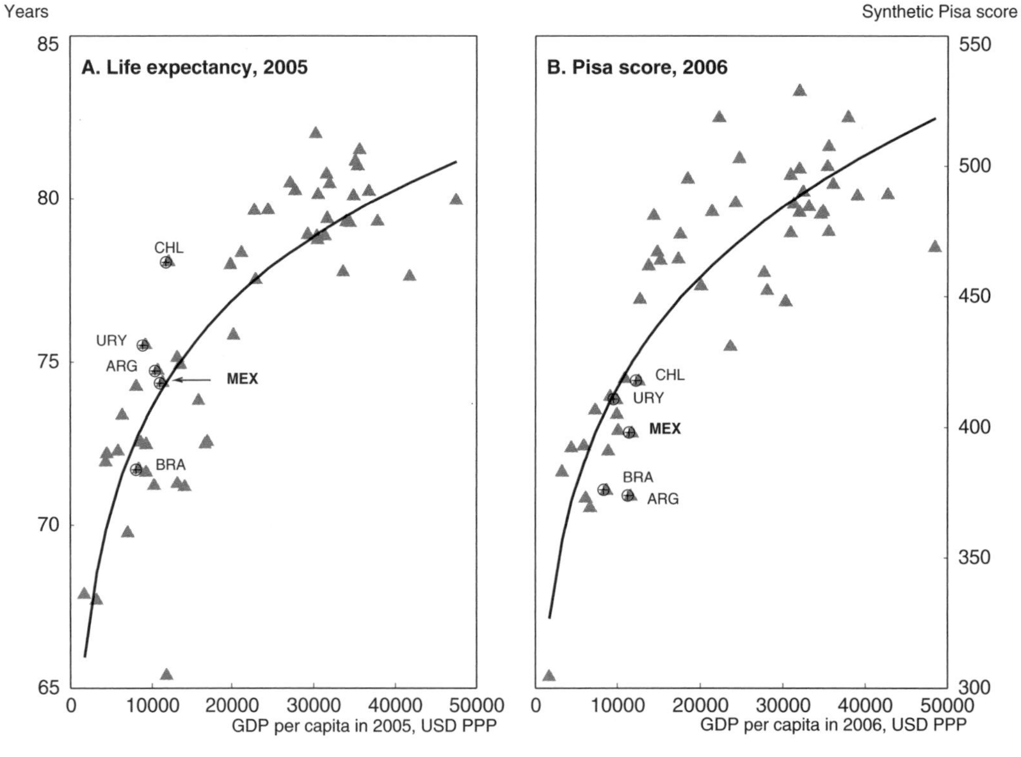

Source: World Bank WDI database; OECD PISA Results.

StatLink ⧉ http://dx.doi.org/10.1787/684136825556

In addition to below average outcomes by international standards, inequality in health and education results across social groups and federal states is high. The ratio of child mortality for mothers without education to mothers with secondary education is one of the highest in the world (WHO, 2007) and child mortality in the poorest federal states is around twice the rate in the richest ones (Figure 3.2). Similarly, results on the standardised PISA tests of student performance display one of the strongest correlations with socioeconomic background of students among OECD countries (OECD, 2007a). They vary by around 80 points between the socioeconomically most advanced states and those that are most backward, as measured by the PISA index of economic, social and cultural status (ESCS) (Figure 3.2). This corresponds roughly to two school years.[1]

Figure 3.2. **Health and education outcomes by state**

2007

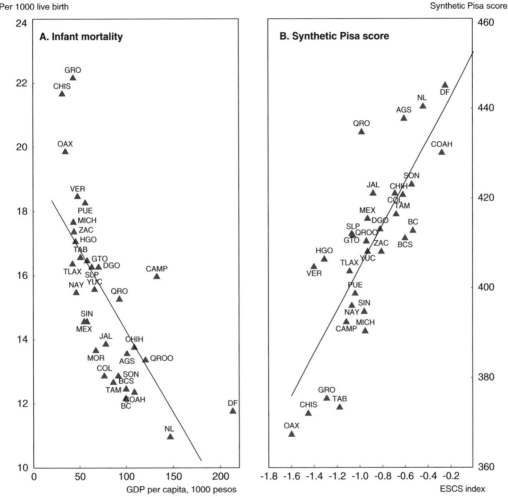

Source: OECD, National Accounts and Analytical databasef; Anexo Estadístico del Segundo Informe del Gobierno.

StatLink ᕝᓏᔲ http://dx.doi.org/10.1787/684157156232

The inequality in health and education outcomes across social groups and federal states reflects incomplete coverage, low quality of services for parts of the population, and fragmentation in services provision. Only two thirds of children complete lower secondary school, and one third of the population, mostly in low income groups, has no health insurance. Weak outcomes on standardised student tests point to problems with the quality of education. In health care, the fragmentation into several separate systems that vertically integrate financing, insurance and provision functions contributes to inefficiencies, for example by duplicating facilities and by increasing administrative costs.

Several reforms to improve social outcomes are under way so that social spending is likely to increase in the near term despite tight budgets. Public spending on health and education in Mexico is more than a quarter of total government expenditures, which is close to the OECD average (Figure 3.3).[2] Further spending pressures will arise from the plan to achieve universal health insurance by 2011. In education, a voluntary agreement between the government and the main teachers' union aims to improve the quality in primary and secondary education, including by increasing spending on school infrastructure.

Figure 3.3. **Government spending**[1]

2006

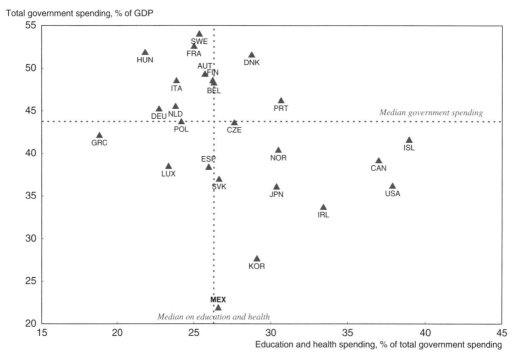

1. Refers to general government.

Source: OECD, National Accounts and Analytical database; Anexo Estadístico del Segundo Informe del Gobierno.

StatLink ⬛🔗 *http://dx.doi.org/10.1787/684176806415*

While additional spending may help if it is well targeted, improving social outcomes will result primarily from increasing the efficiency of existing spending. Using an international comparison of health and education spending, this chapter suggests that there is great potential for improving value for money. It first assesses lack of efficiency of social outlays in Mexico and then discusses potential causes of weak performance. It then reviews ongoing reforms and suggests a number of policies to get better results for the pesos spent on social needs. This is particularly important in the current context of tightening budget constraints with oil and non-oil revenues likely to decline sharply in 2009 and remaining low in 2010, as growth is set to be negative in 2009 with only a tepid recovery in 2010.

Health spending

The structure of the Mexican health system

The Mexican health care system is fragmented into numerous, unconnected providers. The various social security institutes (such as IMSS, ISSSTE and PEMEX) cover about 40% of the population, while the "popular health insurance" scheme (*Seguro Popular*) introduced in 2004 and run by the Ministry of Health (MoH) account for another 25%.[3] The *Seguro Popular* works through decentralised state health services (SHS), which also provide health services to the uninsured population against an income-related user fee (see Box 3.1). Horizontal integration between the different schemes is weak.Affiliates to one scheme cannot, in general, access services provided through the others, and regulation, financing and provision functions are vertically integrated within each scheme (Table 3.1). In addition, there are several non-contributory schemes (such as IMSS-Oportunidades and the health component of Oportunidades) that cater to the uninsured population, as well as private insurers and providers.

Financing of the various schemes is complicated and out-of-pocket spending as a share of total spending is the highest in the OECD.[4] The private insurers are fully financed through affiliates' fees, while the social security schemes rely on a combination of employer and employee contributions and a transfer from the federal government budget.[5] The *Seguro Popular* is financed through federal and state subsidies and a small income-related family fee. Part of the uninsured population has access to a programme providing health care services free of charge in remote areas that are without access to other health care facilities (IMSS-Oportunidades). Most of the uninsured resort to state health facilities against payment of income-related user fees and pay out-of-pocket for services and pharmaceutical drugs in the private sector.

Box 3.1. **Seguro Popular**

Objectives

- Reduce the incidence of catastrophic health expenditure.[1]
- Universal health insurance coverage by 2010, which was recently extended to 2011.

Means

- Basic health insurance package, which covers 266 interventions including primary care and general hospital care (2009 data) and is managed at the state level.
- Fund for Protection against Catastrophic Expenditures (FPGC), which covers 49 high-cost tertiary care interventions (2009 data) and is managed at the federal level to pool risks.
- Health Insurance for a New Generation (since 2007), which covers 116 interventions for newborn children (2009 data) that are not covered by the basic packages of social security or *Seguro Popular*.
- The Strategy for a Healthy Pregnancy covers 14 interventions for pregnant women (2009 data).

Financing

- Central government contribution (0.6% of GDP): fixed premium per family (*Social Quota*) which is equivalent to the one payed to IMSS and ISSSTE plus adjustment for health risks and needs (*Federal Solidarity Contribution*). The *Federal Solidarity Contribution* is compared to the amount the state receives as an earmarked grant for health services and additional resources are only disbursed if the *Federal Solidarity Contribution* is larger than the current earmarked grant.
- State contribution (*State Solidarity Contribution*): half the annual *Social Quota*.
- Family contribution. Fixed proportion of income capped at 5% of income. Lowest two income deciles are exempted.

1. A household faces catastrophic health expenditure when the share of out-of-pocket health expenditure in disposable income exceeds a critical threshold, usually 30%.

Table 3.1. **The Mexican health care system**

Functions	Private insurers	Social security institutes			Seguro Popular	Uninsured	
Regulation (standards, quality) Financing (contributions, fee for service) Provision	Commercial enterprises	IMSS	ISSSTE	Others (PEMEX, Navy, SEMAR, other public)	MoH, SHS	IMSS-Oportunidades	MoH, SHS
Percentage of population	2%	32%	6%	2%	25%	10%	23%

Note: All figures except *Seguro Popular* and IMSS-Oportunidades are estimated using the coverage rates reported in the 2005 Population Census and population projections for 2007. The *Seguro Popular* coverage rate is calculated using total population covered by March 2009 and the IMSS-Oportunidades estimates refer to figures submitted to the MoH by IMSS-Oportunidades in 2007. Coverage differs depending on whether census data or administrative data are used. According to administrative data 48% of the population is insured at IMSS and 10% at ISSSTE.
Source: MoH submission.

Efficiency frontier analysis

The efficiency of health spending can be analysed by comparing the distance of health outcomes from an efficiency frontier. The frontier is obtained through Data Envelopment Analysis (DEA) that relates monetary and non-monetary inputs into the health system to health indicators (for details see Box 3.2 and Annex 3.A1). Following Joumard *et al.* (2008) outcomes of the health system are proxied by life expectancy at birth. Total health spending per capita, GDP per capita, and fruit and vegetable consumption per capita are used as input variables. Deviations from the estimated efficiency frontier indicate inefficiencies.

Mexico is among the least efficient within the OECD on the indicator of life expectancy at birth and about average among emerging markets (Figure 3.4). Although it is relatively far from the OECD frontier, it scores better than Poland and the Slovak Republic, at similar income levels, and better than some of the higher income OECD members – Denmark and the United States. Among non-OECD emerging markets Mexico's efficiency score is about average but it falls behind Argentina, Brazil and Chile. Although quantitative measures of potential efficiency gains have to be taken with a grain of salt due to potentially omitted determinants of health outcomes, the DEA suggests large potential gains for Mexico from

Figure 3.4. **Efficiency of the health system**

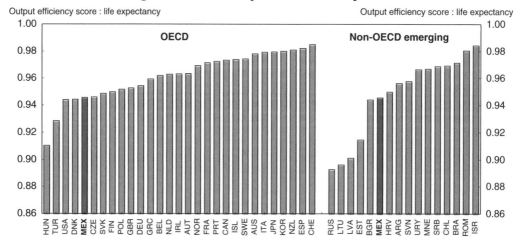

Source: World Bank, World Development Indicators database; FAO, Faostat database.

StatLink http://dx.doi.org/10.1787/684184362517

Box 3.2. **Measuring efficiency of social spending**

The analysis conducted for this chapter estimates an efficiency frontier that relates outcomes of the health and education system to monetary and non-monetary inputs through Data Envelopment Analysis (DEA). The method uses linear programming techniques to construct a frontier from the most efficient observations, which "envelop" the less efficient ones (Figure 3.5).

Figure 3.5. **Efficiency frontiers**
Non-increasing returns to scale

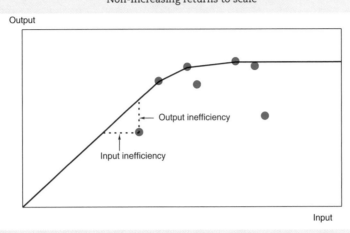

Source: Sutherland et al. (2007).

StatLink ⟶ http://dx.doi.org/10.1787/684188563804

The method distinguishes between input and output efficiency, and technical and allocative efficiency. Input efficiency requires the use of a minimum bundle of inputs to produce a given output, while output efficiency requires the maximum amount of output from a given bundle of inputs. Allocative efficiency is more relevant than technical efficiency as it requires cost minimisation or benefit maximisation.[1] This section uses output efficiency in the allocative sense to measure efficiency of social spending in Mexico. This is the appropriate concept for the Mexican case in that, rather than minimising costs at the current level of health and education outcomes, the objective of the Mexican authorities is to reduce the gap in outcomes with the other OECD countries at the current level of costs. Technical efficiency allows conclusions on the efficient use of physical health inputs to be drawn but not on the efficiency of spending.

While the DEA analysis provides a neat summary measure of efficiency of spending, it has a number of drawbacks that have to be addressed in its practical implementation.

- **Sensitivity to outliers.** A country that has an atypical combination of inputs and outputs is likely to be classified as efficient because there are no appropriate comparator countries in the sample. The efficiency analysis in this chapter therefore includes 15 non-OECD emerging countries for which data are available in addition to OECD members.

- **Sensitivity to small samples.** If the sample is small, the efficiency level is likely to be overestimated because the most efficient country is likely to be excluded from the sample. The efficiency scores reported in this chapter are therefore corrected for small sample bias through a statistical procedure (see Annex 3.A1).

- **Sensitivity to the number of included inputs and the form of the efficiency frontier.** Only a limited number of inputs can be included in the estimation and an assumption on economies of scale in production has to be made. The efficiency scores reported in this chapter are robust to various sensitivity checks on included inputs and economies of scale. On grounds of economic plausibility, only efficiency scores using the assumption of non-increasing returns to scale are reported.

1. Note that a country may be technically efficient but may not be minimising costs.

improved efficiency. Life expectancy at birth could be increased by over 4 years at the current level of health care spending if resources were spent more efficiently.

Sources of inefficiencies

The low efficiency of health spending in Mexico reflects a number of structural factors. Compared to better performers, Mexico stands out with low health insurance coverage of the population – around one third of Mexicans are not covered. Along with the United States it is the only OECD country that does not have universal health insurance.[6] Insurance status is closely related to health outcomes as the uninsured are less likely to receive appropriate preventive care, which often leads to less successful and more costly treatment when sick (Docteur and Oxley, 2003). For instance, cancers among the uninsured are more likely to be diagnosed at later stages, when treatment is less successful and more costly. The uninsured are also less likely to receive timely care for chronic conditions which may lead to further deterioration in their health and more costly interventions. For instance, uninsured individuals are less likely to receive drug therapy for high blood pressure, resulting eventually in a more costly heart condition.

Another important source of inefficiency is the high fragmentation of the system. Several social security institutes, private insurers, federal and state health services each have their own vertically integrated service providers with no access to each others' services. This has resulted in a costly duplication of health administration and infrastructure, curtailment of patient choice and lack of competition between providers. Chile, for instance, where the functions of insurer and provider of care have been split, spends less on health care per capita than Mexico but has a higher life expectancy at birth and a lower child mortality rate.

The weak outcomes are also affected by the bias in coverage against the lower income groups. In 2006 only about 20% of the poorest income group (lowest decile) were insured compared to about 70% in the highest deciles (Figure 3.6).[7] Only salaried workers in the formal sector have access to health insurance through the social security institutes, whereas low-income non-salaried workers or workers in the informal sector are either uninsured or have access to the voluntary health insurance scheme (*Seguro Popular*). The introduction of *Seguro*

Figure 3.6. **Health insurance coverage by income decile**

2006

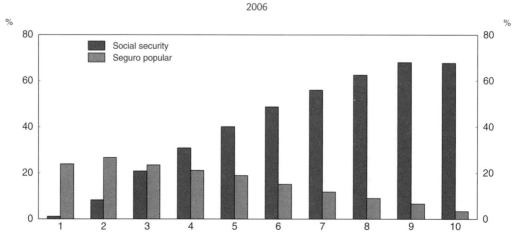

Source: ENIGH Household Income Survey 2006.

StatLink ⏎ *http://dx.doi.org/10.1787/684203367114*

Popular in 2004 improved coverage and reduced regressivity. However, as its enrolment is still only about a third of that of the social security institutes, overall coverage remains higher for the richer part of the population. Given that health insurance status is positively associated with health outcomes (Hadley, 2003), increasing insurance coverage among the lower income groups would have a large pay-off in terms of overall population health outcomes.

The weak outcomes may also reflect lower insurance coverage and spending per capita in states with lower incomes. The bias in total public per capita spending is partly due to higher social security coverage in the richer federal states (Figure 3.7) and partly to the lower own resources allocated to health care in the poorer states that have lower tax collection capacities. The earmarked federal transfer to the states (the *Fondo de Aportaciones para los Servicios de Salud, FASSA*) used to be regressive before the introduction of *Seguro Popular*. Currently there are no clear distributional effects, mainly because the transfer now depends on the number of families enrolled in *Seguro Popular*. The fact that intensity of resource use is higher in the states with scarce resources suggests that there may be excess

Figure 3.7. **Social security coverage by state**
2006

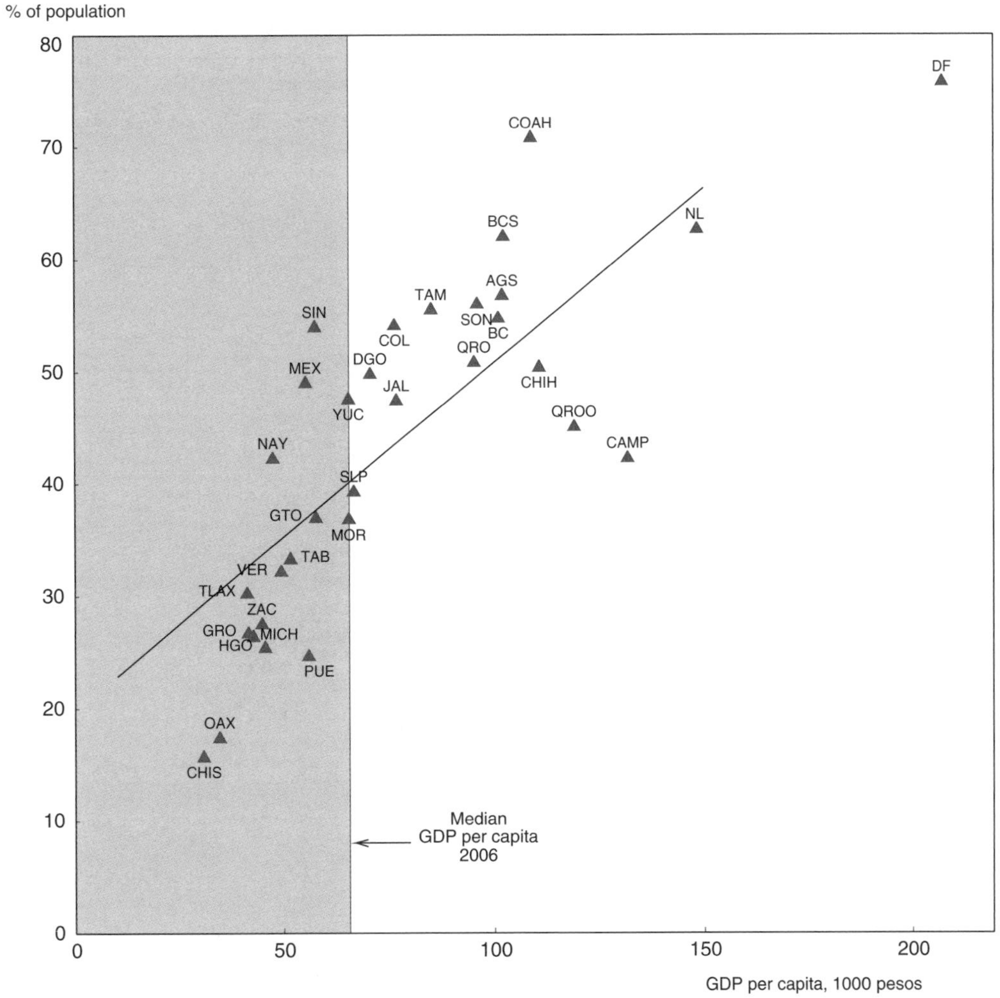

Source: OECD, National Accounts and Analytical database; Ministry of Health, Boletín de Informaciòn Estadística.
StatLink ⟡ http://dx.doi.org/10.1787/684244603127

demand and rationing of patients in some states and oversupply in others (Figure 3.8). This could be addressed by better linking public spending on health to states' needs.

The fragmentation of the health system into several unconnected networks has led to under- or overuse of facilities. There may be excess supply of care provision in one network and excess demand in another. On the supply side, this results in inefficiencies due to the non-equalisation of marginal costs. On the demand side, inefficiencies arise from implicit rationing of patients in the over-utilised scheme. For example, utilisation rates of MoH and ISSSTE facilities compared to those of IMSS at the state level are very different. In the federal district (mainly Mexico City, DF) discharges per hospital bed in the MoH network are around three times the rate in IMSS (Figure 3.9). This suggests that in the federal district there may be rationing at MoH facilities while those of IMSS may be under-utilised. If MoH patients had access to IMSS facilities overall costs could be reduced by shifting patients to the lowest marginal cost providers, and patients' satisfaction improved by reducing implicit rationing. While there is no general pattern of utilisation rates across MoH and IMSS resources, ISSSTE services appear to be generally underutilised – they are below those of IMSS in most states (Figure 3.9).

Figure 3.8. **Health consumption by state**

2006

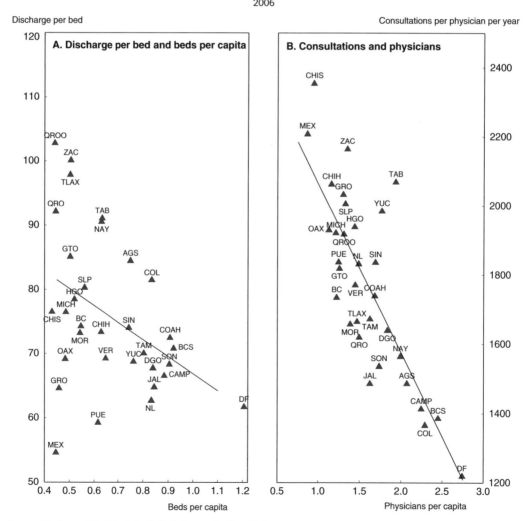

Source: Ministry of Health, Boletín de Informaciòn Estadística.

StatLink ⬛⬛⬛ http://dx.doi.org/10.1787/684245315014

Figure 3.9. **Health consumption by state and network**

2006

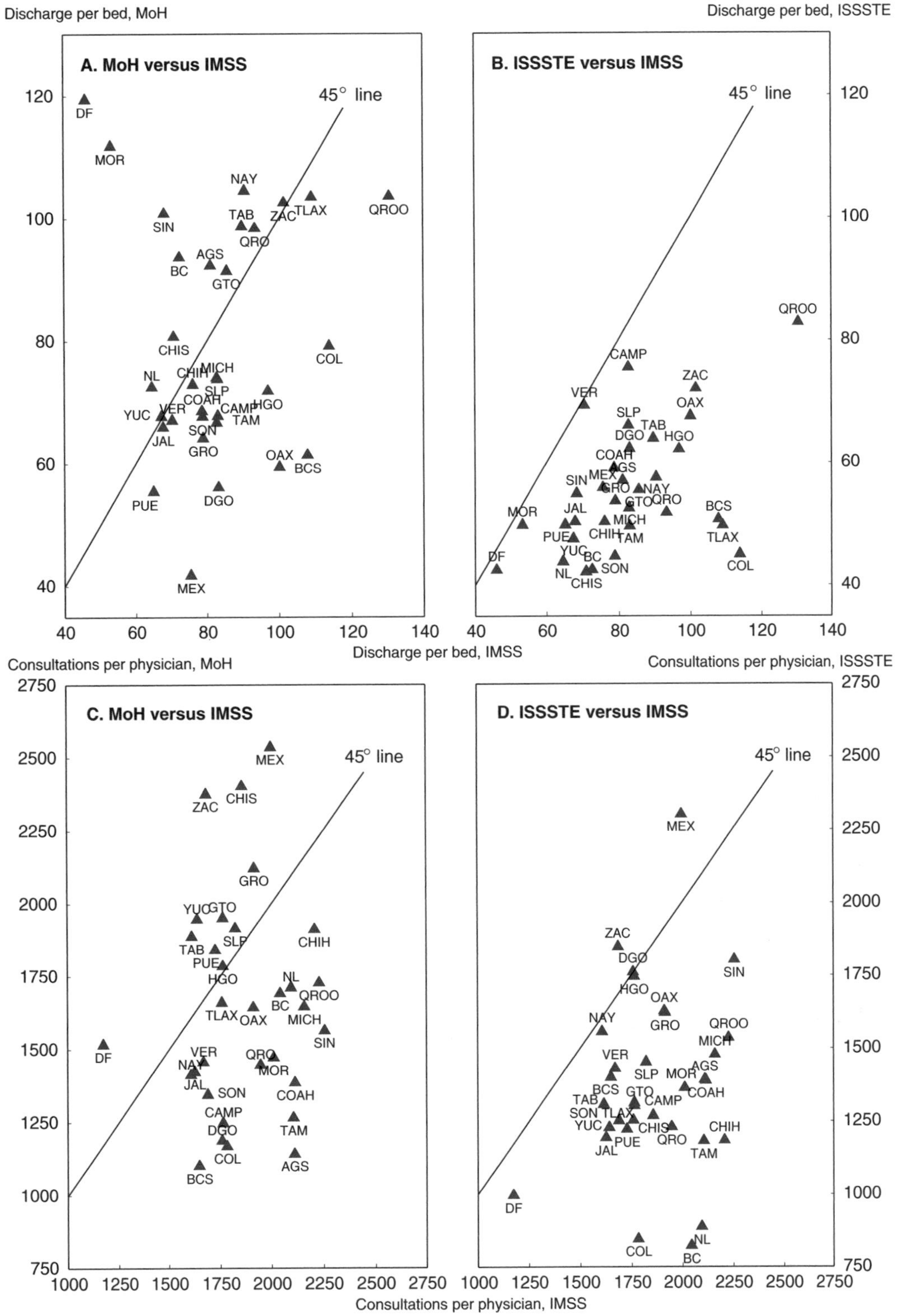

Source: Ministry of Health, Boletín de Informaciòn Estadística.

StatLink ᤁᤐᤁᤛ http://dx.doi.org/10.1787/684287410461

The fragmentation of the Mexican health system also reduces efficiency by increasing administrative costs. The existence of several vertically integrated insurer-providers leads to the duplication of administrative structures and precludes taking advantage of economies of scale in administration. Comparing administrative costs across countries is difficult and quantitative estimates have to be interpreted with caution. However, according to available data, the Mexican health system has the highest relative administrative costs in the OECD (Figure 3.10). To reduce administrative costs in health systems with multiple insurers, other OECD countries have introduced centralised claims management systems. In Turkey, for instance, a reform in 2007 established a centralised claims management system for the existing contributory and non-contributory insurance schemes (OECD, 2009). All providers in Turkey are required to submit claims through this system, which leads to economies of scale in administration and, through standardisation, reduces the administrative burden to both providers and insurers. The introduction of a centralised claims management system would, of course, only make sense if all providers could sell services to all insurers, which, as in Turkey, requires an insurer-provider split (see Box 3.3 on the Turkish reform).[8]

Box 3.3. **Health reform in Turkey**

Pre-reform situation

Before the reform initiated in 2003 the Turkish health system was highly fragmented, both in insurance and in provision. Three separate social security institutes for formal sector workers with differing benefits packages co-existed, with the main social security institute for blue and white-collar workers (SSK) acting both as an insurer and as a provider. Additionally, a programme introduced in 1992 for the poor that were incapable of paying for health services was managed by the Ministry of Health (Green Card). Nevertheless, in 2003 only around 85% of the population was covered by some type of health insurance.

Objectives of the 2003 reform (Health Transformation Programme)

The main objectives of the Health Transformation Programme were i) to establish universal health insurance by making health insurance mandatory and ii) to split insurance and provision functions. Health insurance would be fully subsidised for the poorest parts of the population. The three social security institutes and the Green Card would be merged into a single payer, that would provide the insurance function and contract with both private and public providers.

Current status of the reform

The Social Security and Universal Health Insurance Law was operationalised in October 2008 and health insurance is now mandatory for all Turkish citizens. Premium rates have been set at 12.5% of salaries. Contributions are fully subsidised for poor households and reduced rates apply for non-poor households who were previously holding a Green Card. SSK has given up its provision functions to the Ministry of Health but the Ministry still acts as both insurer (through the management of the Green Card programme) and provider. A unified claims management system has been introduced as a first step towards merging the three social security institutes and the Green Card programme. All providers have to process their claims through this system.

Decentralisation contributes to inefficiencies by further fragmenting the Mexican health care system. Health care provision by the MoH was decentralised to the states in two waves in the 1980s and the 1990s. In this system the central government would only set the overall policy framework (objectives, the regulatory framework, coordination and evaluation) while state authorities organise and operate health care services. The aim was to reduce bureaucratic and highly centralised decision making, which was perceived to be the source of a mismatch between resources and needs. This reform was also expected to improve coordination between providers that serve the uninsured population. However, it has not led to efficiency gains (OECD, 2005) as the MoH tends to have weak regulatory and supervisory powers. There is also lack of coordination between the federal and the state levels, and marked differences in financial resources and management capacities across federal states. The historically-based federal transfers to the states have only recently been reformed, and many states still lack information and management systems for output-based management of their health care facilities. Moreover, the states' autonomy in organising and operating health care services is constrained by the centrally negotiated collective labour contract for health care employees, which limits the funds for non-wage uses. Coordination between IMSS, IMSS-Oportunidades and MoH providers has improved but remains weak, reducing potential efficiency gains.

Compared to best practice countries, the use of block grants to reimburse providers in Mexico can be another source of inefficiencies.[9] Providers are reimbursed based on block grants with no clear link between service provision and financing. Some OECD countries have introduced payments for providers using prospective or pre-negotiated fee-for-service arrangements as a way to improve efficiency (Docteur and Oxley, 2003). This requires a clear split between insurers and providers, with insurers focusing on collecting premiums and purchasing services and providers focusing on providing quality services at minimum cost.

Figure 3.10. **Administrative costs**

As a percentage of total health care spending, 2005

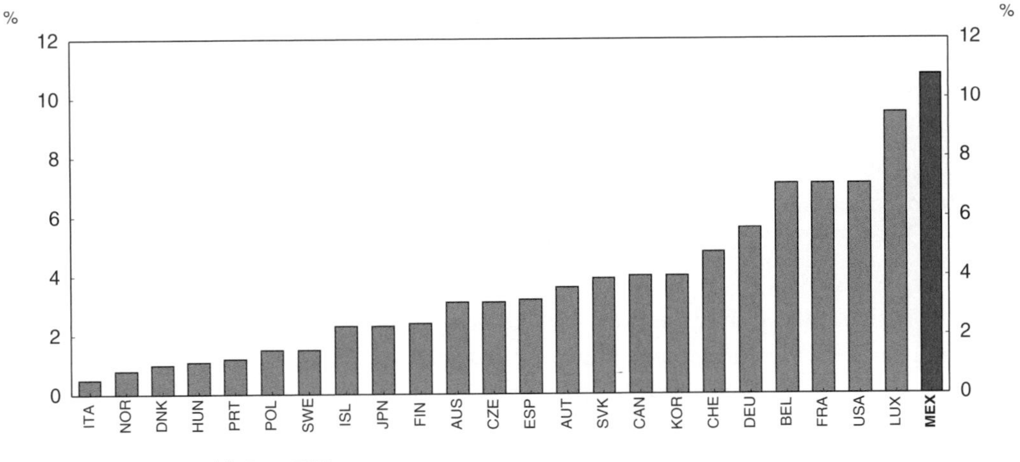

Source: OECD, OECD Health Data 2008.

StatLink ᓕᓕᓕᓚ http://dx.doi.org/10.1787/684322473258

The input-mix can be another source of inefficiencies in the Mexican health care system. As costs of health care services may not be comparable internationally, costs efficiencies are often analyzed with input mix indicators. The low nurses-to-physicians ratio suggests that there is little pressure on hospitals to explore more cost-efficient input mixes (Figure 3.11). Since Mexico has a large number of nurses who are currently not practising in the health sector (Nigenda et al., 2003) this may not reflect a supply constraint.

Figure 3.11. **Ratio of nurses to physicians**

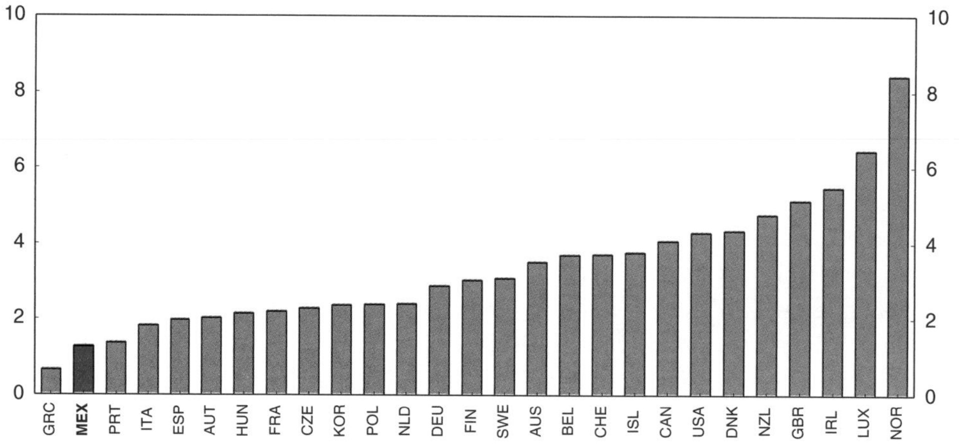

Source: OECD, OECD Health Data 2008.

StatLink http://dx.doi.org/10.1787/684346560211

Finally, the multitude of programmes targeted at the currently uninsured may lead to targeting errors and inefficiencies. Around one third of IMSS-Oportunidades users, a non-contributory scheme for the poor run by the main social security institute, are also insured by the main social security provider (IMSS).[10] There is also some overlap between IMSS and *Seguro Popular*, which results in higher fiscal costs through the double payment of the subsidy per enrollee both insurers receive from the federal government.

Recent reforms

Several reforms have aimed to improve efficiency in the Mexican health system. The last major reform was the introduction of the System for Social Protection in Health (*Sistema de Protección Social en Salud*, SPSS) in 2004, which was a continuation of earlier reform efforts in 1995-97. The main longer-term objectives of the reforms have included policies to address many of the problems identified above: achieving more horizontal integration between the various insurance schemes, expanding coverage of the currently uninsured population, separating insurance and provider functions, and achieving more equity in financing (Frenk *et al.*, 2006), and strengthening the oversight role of the federal MoH.

Despite reforms, public spending on health remains regressive.[11] The correlation between health care spending per capita and GDP per capita at the state level has become slightly less regressive between 2003 (the year before the reform) and the latest available year (2007) (Figure 3.12).[12] While a 10% positive deviation of GDP per capita from the average was associated with 5.9% per capita supplementary spending on health care before the reform, it is still associated with 5.3%. The small size of these figures suggests that there remains considerable room for making spending more equitable, notably through efforts to increase affiliation rates to *Seguro Popular* in the poorer states.

The *Seguro Popular*, the main pillar of the 2004 reform, aims at achieving universal coverage by 2011 through voluntary enrolment. It also aims at reducing the existing segmentation of the system by letting the *Seguro Popular* contract services from the SHS, the social security institutes or private providers, although in practice most of the services

Figure 3.12. **Public health spending by state**

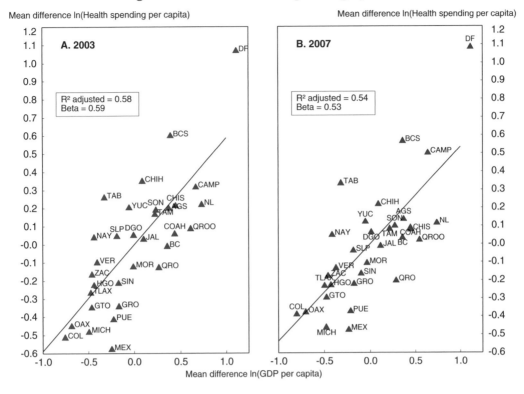

Source: Ministry of Health, Boletín de Informaciòn Estadística.

StatLink ᵐᵃ⁵ᵖ http://dx.doi.org/10.1787/684412270882

are still contracted from the SHS. The oversight role of the MoH is strengthened through certification requirements for providers, new infrastructure and through an expansion of its competencies in evaluation and assessment. The reform further aims at reducing the regressivity of the earmarked grants to the states and better linking resource allocation and needs. This is achieved by the new *Social Quota* and *Federal Solidarity Contribution* funds that are currently mainly distributed according to the number of families affiliated to *Seguro Popular*. Finally, funding for health-related public goods, such as oversight, evaluation, research or community health services, is separated from funding for personal health services. The aim is to prevent public health activities from being neglected or under-financed during the reform process.

The *Seguro Popular* has been successful in increasing coverage and improving the composition of spending. Health insurance coverage has increased from around 40% in 2004 to around 65% of the population in 2008, with the *Seguro Popular* now covering more than 25%.[13] This should gradually improve health indicators. In view of the above analysis, channeling new funds to insure the uninsured population who may delay treatment in case of an ailment, which increases future costs of curative care, should be an efficient way of allocating health care spending. Since 2001 there has also been an important shift in the composition of spending away from personnel towards operations (mainly pharmaceutical drugs) and investment, and spending on prevention has been stepped up substantially.

The *Seguro Popular* has been ineffective in reducing fragmentation, but recent policies are going in the right direction. A recently launched programme, for instance, allows pregnant women to use any healthcare facility regardless of their insurance and a master plan for health infrastructure is being developed under which newly built healthcare facilities will be shared by the different insurers, as needed. IMSS and *Seguro Popular* are estimating costs of providing services in order to be able to bill each other and have teamed up with ISSSTE to negotiate prices on patented drugs with pharmaceutical companies for the first time in 2008. Nevertheless, progress in reducing fragmentation has been slow. The *Seguro Popular* still contracts most of its services from the SHS and the social security institutes grant the *Seguro Popular* only very limited access to their health facilities.

Problems with the implementation of the *Seguro Popular* suggest that its targets may not be met as envisaged, and that the potential for improving outcomes may not be realised. A report of the Auditor General (Auditoría, 2007) noted that the *Seguro Popular* does not systematically monitor performance on catastrophic health expenditure. The problem has been partly addressed. A 2008 evaluation found that catastrophic health expenditure appeared to be lower for *Seguro Popular* enrollees than for the uninsured (INS, 2008). But as it is not clear from the report whether a causal interpretation of the figures can actually be made, further evaluation seems warranted.[14] Secondly, the Auditor General points out that the *Seguro Popular* is unlikely to achieve universal coverage by it original target date of 2010, mainly because the MoH may have underestimated the demographic growth of the target population. It is currently estimated to be around 12.6 million families in 2010, but Auditoría (2007) thinks it will grow to 14 million. Thus even if the MoH target is met, 1.4 million families (around 5% of the population) would remain without health insurance coverage. More generally, there appears to be a high degree of uncertainty about the exact size of *Seguro Popular's* target population because a centralised roster of individuals covered by any of the various insurers has not been set up. Finally, the report points out that the increases in the number of interventions included in the basic insurance package of *Seguro Popular* have led to a deficit of 12 billion pesos in 2005 as income only covered around 60% of costs.[15] If this trend continues, implementation may be confronted with budgetary problems, which may be further aggravated by the states' practice of waiving the family contribution for those that are not in the two lowest income deciles (Gakidou *et al.*, 2006).

The social security institutes haves voiced concerns that the introduction of the *Seguro Popular* may lead to a deterioration of their risk pools (IMSS, 2008). If younger and healthier individuals prefer the less comprehensive but cheaper *Seguro Popular* package, older and less healthy individuals may select into the higher-cost social security because of its more comprehensive health care package. To date, there is no empirical evidence to back this hypothesis, and its practical relevance may be limited by the fact that the *Seguro Popular* and the social security packages are not directly comparable due to additional benefits in the latter.

A potentially more serious risk to the success of the *Seguro Popular* in achieving universal coverage is voluntary enrolment. OECD countries that have recently adopted universal health insurance have made it mandatory to avoid adverse selection issues. In a voluntary scheme, such as *Seguro Popular*, the healthiest individuals may not take up insurance in order to save on insurance premia. This is not an issue for those in the two lowest income deciles since they are exempted from paying the premia. However, adverse selection may affect the higher income deciles and could, through a deterioration of the programme's risk pool, eventually undermine its financial sustainability. To date no empirical evidence is available on the health characteristics of *Seguro Popular* affiliates as compared to the uninsured population. An evaluation would be warranted to determine the existence and extent of adverse selection into *Seguro Popular* and to devise appropriate policy responses.

Some have raised concerns that the rise in the number of non-contributory social programmes in Mexico may undermine the financial sustainability of the social security institutes.[16] Employees and employers may have an incentive to shift employment from salaried employment in the formal sector to non-salaried employment in the informal sector to save on social security contributions. The family contribution to the *Seguro Popular* is significantly lower than the wage-based social security one. This could erode the tax base of the social security institutes. However, a simple inspection of the time series of IMSS enrollees does not indicate any clear changes since the introduction of the *Seguro Popular* (Figure 3.13) suggesting that there are other benefits of being part of the formal sector. The package of health care interventions of *Seguro Popular* is less comprehensive than the social security package, which also work-risk, disability and life insurance, retirement pensions, daycare centers, sports facilities and a housing fund. The increase in income from shifting to non-salaried employment could also be subject to income taxes, lowering the net benefit to the parties concerned. Since social security contributions are deductible from income taxes and non-salaried employment is in principle subject to income taxes, the after-tax increase in income is lower than the difference between social security contributions and the *Seguro Popular* family contribution. Finally, the fact that social security is both explicitly and implicitly subsidised but formal employment covers only 38% of the workforce (Levy, 2008) suggests that there may be other barriers to formal employment such as rigidities in the formal labour market.[17]

Figure 3.13. **Enrollees by network**

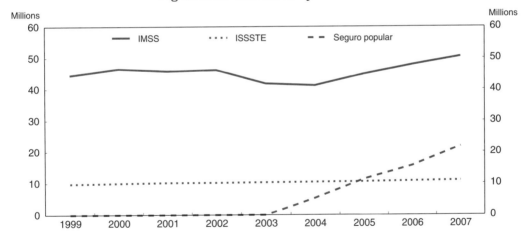

Source: Ministry of Health.

StatLink http://dx.doi.org/10.1787/684412541216

Although the impact of *Seguro Popular* on social security enrolment seems to be weak, at the margin 10-20% of workers tend to switch from the informal to the formal sector or *vice versa* every year (Levy 2008). For these marginal workers the trade-off between higher take-home wages and social security benefits may well matter. This could partly be addressed by not waiving the *Seguro Popular* insurance premia for non-poor households in contrast to current practice, which would make non-salaried employment in the informal sector financially less attractive to them.

What can be done to improve efficiency in the Mexican health system?

Efforts to achieve universal health insurance coverage through *Seguro Popular* should be continued. Apart from improving the overall efficiency of the health system with preventive and timely care, the *Seguro Popular* seeks to reduce inequality in health outcomes across socioeconomic groups and federal states by channelling additional public funds to the poorest families without social security coverage and to the states where the needs are the greatest.

Discussions on making health insurance coverage *mandatory* should be initiated as soon as possible. Under mandatory health insurance all uninsured citizens would have to subscribe to a health insurance policy, either private or *Seguro Popular*. This would reduce adverse selection and ensure full coverage if potentially important enforcement problems can be overcome. In the longer term, the authorities should consider financing a higher share of public health spending through general taxation with the aim of reducing the duality in financing of the social security institutes mainly through payroll contributions and *Seguro Popular* mainly through general taxation.

The efficiency of the health system could also be improved by introducing a clear split between insurer and provision functions. Any insurer should be allowed to contract with any provider. This would reduce the cost of provision to the insurers who would have an incentive to choose the providers with the lowest cost, thereby encouraging providers themselves to become more efficient. With a split between insurers and providers, economies of scale in administration could be reaped by requiring all providers to submit claims through a centralised claims management system.

Further improvements in the efficiency of the health system could be achieved by improving the targeting of *Seguro Popular* and IMSS-Oportunidades. Health insurance through *Seguro Popular* should be fully subsidised for poor households but the requirement for non-poor households to pay their family contribution should be enforced. Overlap between IMSS and *Seguro Popular* should be eliminated by setting up a centralised roster of enrollees.

Efficiency of spending on primary and secondary education

The Mexican education system

The Mexican education system has three basic levels, as in most other OECD countries (Box 3.4). While the coverage of primary education is close to 100%, that for 15-year old students, at 64%, is low compared to peers (OECD, 2008b) despite schooling being compulsory until the age of 15. Education quality is another problem, as indicated by the poor PISA scores, which would likely be even lower if the low enrolment was accounted for. Higher education only reaches a small part of the population. Although the share of education spending in GDP is higher than the OECD average (6.5% against 5.8%), it is low in per student terms (adjusted for PPP). This partly reflects Mexico's age structure, which is younger than in most OECD countries (Figures 3.14 and 3.15). At the same time, the low PISA scores for those currently in schools suggest that resources could have been spent more efficiently. Improving quality and enlarging coverage are difficult tasks in an environment of tight budget constraints from declining oil revenues and competing social

Box 3.4. **The Mexican education system**

The Mexican education system is structured into basic education (*educación básica*, pre-school, primary and lower secondary), upper secondary education (*educación media superior*) and higher education (*educación superior*). Children attend the three grades of pre-school between the ages of 3 and 5, the six grades of primary school between the age of 6 and 11, and the three grades of lower secondary education between the ages of 12-14. Regular schools are complemented by special community schools (around 10% of students enrolled in basic education) that cater to students in marginalised areas or those with large indigenous populations, the so-called *Telesecundaria* (around 20% of students enrolled in lower secondary education) that provides lower secondary learning via television in remote areas, and technical lower secondary education (*secundaria técnica*, around 25% of lower secondary students). School attendance is mandatory until the completion of lower secondary education. Upper secondary education lasts, in general, three years and includes a general or technical baccalaureate (*bacchillerato general* and *bachillerato tecnológico*) or vocational training (*profesional técnico*). After upper secondary education students can move on to undergraduate (3-6 years) and post-graduate (1-4 years) university studies. During the 2007-08 school year around 25 million students were enrolled in basic education, 4 million in upper secondary and 3 million in higher education (INEE, 2008). Public spending shares were, respectively, 66%, 14% and 20% (OECD, 2008b). Around 90% of students in primary and lower-secondary education go to public schools.

Figure 3.14. **PISA score and education spending per student**

2007

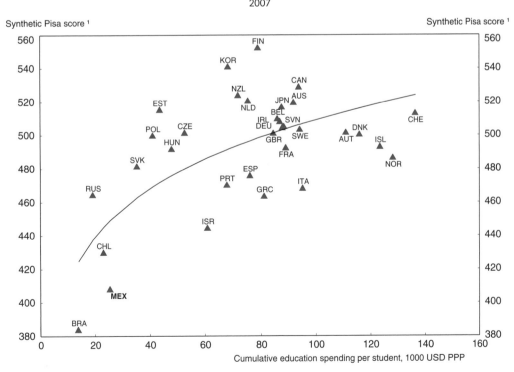

1. The synthetic PISA score combines the scores on the reading, mathematics and science scale through factor analysis.

Source: OECD, PISA Results 2006.

StatLink ⇒ http://dx.doi.org/10.1787/684413472040

Figure 3.15. **Secondary enrolment at age 15**

2006

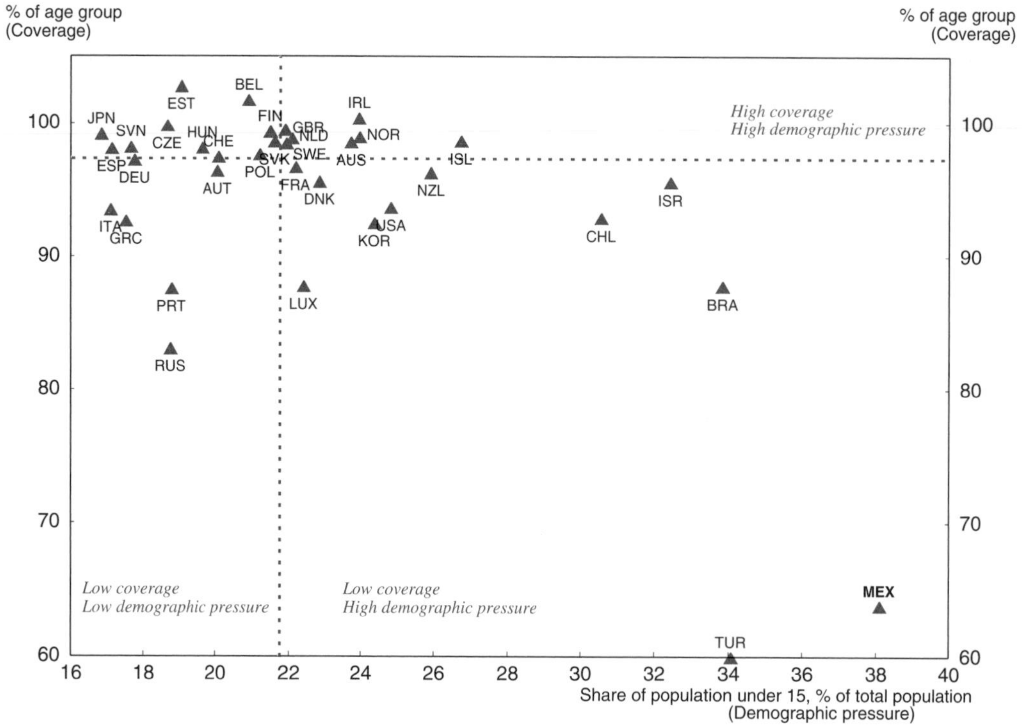

Source: OECD, Education database.

StatLink http://dx.doi.org/10.1787/684437000415

needs. This underlines the importance of improving efficiency of current spending on schools.

To assess the efficiency of education spending, this chapter focuses on secondary school coverage and quality of education, which are the main challenges in Mexico's education system. Covering the one third of children currently not completing lower-secondary education is an important challenge and together with improving education quality are likely to demand more resources. Part of these can be met by a more efficient use of existing outlays.

Efficiency frontier analysis

The results from the efficiency frontier analysis show that Mexico is one of the least efficient among both emerging and OECD countries in education spending (Figure 3.16). The outcome variable used in the analysis is a synthetic PISA score that combines the reading, mathematics and science scores through factor analysis. The input is education spending per student, and the PISA ESCS index is used as an environmental variable (Annex 3.A1 for details). Mexico has one of the lowest scores among OECD and non-OECD emerging markets and ranks between Argentina and Chile in Latin America. Subject to the usual caveats, the scores suggest that Mexico could increase its synthetic PISA score by 74 points at the current level of education spending if resources were spent efficiently.

Mexico's PISA scores are also low across the different subject areas. The results on reading are about 80% of the OECD average with no improvement since the first PISA

Figure 3.16. **Efficiency of education spending**

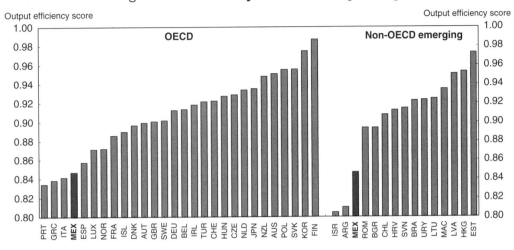

Source: OECD, PISA Results 2006; World Bank, WDI database.

StatLink ᴍᴤ🔗 http://dx.doi.org/10.1787/684445426166

evaluation in 2000.[18] Progress has been better in maths and Mexico increased from 77% to 81% of the OECD average since 2003. On the science test, which was included for the first time in 2006, results are at around 82% of the OECD average. This means that Mexican students are on average 2-3 years behind the OECD average. The results also show that around half of Mexican students do not reach basic proficiency levels, against an OECD average of around a fifth.[19]

The Mexican PISA scores are also highly dispersed according to income levels. The share of the variation in PISA scores explained by the ESCS index is one of the highest in the OECD (OECD, 2007a). The importance of socioeconomic background is also evidenced in PISA scores across states. The performance gap between the high-income federal district and some more advanced OECD economies, such as Greece, Italy or Portugal, is small, while it remains large for poorer federal states, such as Oaxaca or Chiapas. The main challenge in improving overall educational outcomes in Mexico is to provide equal learning opportunities for all students, which should help increase test scores for the large number of students from weak socioeconomic backgrounds.

Sources of inefficiencies

The outcomes are influenced by an allocation of federal resources that does not take into account states' needs or performance. Federal transfers are based on cost shares that existed before the 1998 fiscal reform (Law on Fiscal Coordination), which has tended to favour some of the higher-income states (Joumard, 2005). However, needs for additional resources are generally higher in the poorer income states. According to SEP (2007), more than 150 students have to share one computer with internet access in low-income Chiapas, but less than 25 have to do so in richer Colima. Even though recent studies have shown that additional resources do not mechanically result in performance improvements (Hanushek, 2003), re-balancing the federal transfer in favour of the lower-income states is likely to improve efficiency if additional funds are made conditional on performance improvements. In the United States, the recent "No Child Left Behind" initiative makes additional funds available for states that improve academic achievement (see Box 3.5).

> ### Box 3.5. **"No Child Left Behind" and additional funds for US states**
>
> The "No Child Left Behind" initiative gives US states more flexibility in the use of federal funds in return for complying to strict accountability requirements, and makes additional funds available in return for improvements in academic achievement. States can request even more flexibility if they submit a five-year performance improvement plan to the Secretary of Education and if they agree to be regularly evaluated during the course of the plan. States that fall short of the performance improvement objectives in the plan are sanctioned. Additional funds are made available through the "Achievement in Education" fund rewarding the states that have made the greatest progress in improving academic achievement, as measured by states' and national assessments.

Quality of education may also be influenced by the allocation of resources in favour of labour versus capital. Countries with high shares of non-wage spending in total education spending generally achieve higher DEA efficiency scores (Figure 3.17).[20] If there are complementarities between labour and capital, disproportionately high spending on either can result in an inefficient input mix. For instance, increasing spending on teachers' salaries may not result in improved outcomes if it is not accompanied by increased spending on teaching materials, school infrastructure and training. The share of these non-wage spending items in total education spending in Mexico is one of the lowest in the OECD. Allocating new spending predominantly to non-wage items would reduce the undercapitalisation of the Mexican school system and could improve efficiency.

Figure 3.17. **Non-wage spending and efficiency**

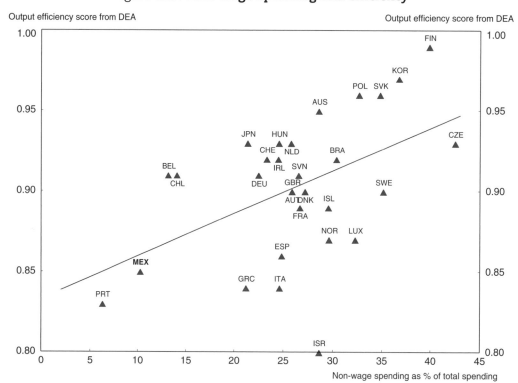

Source: OECD, Education at a Glance 2008.

StatLink 🔗 http://dx.doi.org/10.1787/684461707460

Uneven teacher quality across states is another important determinant of education outcomes. Selecting the most qualified teachers and setting the appropriate incentives for them is crucial to improving the efficiency of schools. In Mexico, teachers started to be selected based on nation-wide entry examinations only in 2008-2009. Some federal states have used state entry examinations, others have shared responsibilities or relied on the teachers' union to fill new positions (Guichard, 2005). This has resulted in a high dispersion in secondary school teachers' professional qualifications across federal states (Figure 3.18). In some states only a third of secondary school teachers hold a university degree, whereas in others the share is close to 80%.[21] The introduction of a nation-wide entry examination for the selection of teachers in the *Alianza* is an overdue and welcome measure to improve the quality of teaching in all federal states (see below). However, its implementation in 2008 faced resistance from teachers in some states.

Figure 3.18. **Secondary school teachers with university degree**

As % of all teachers

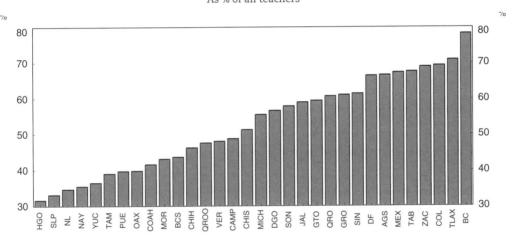

Source: Secretarìa de Educacìon Pùblica.

StatLink ᵃ⁄ₛ http://dx.doi.org/10.1787/684464353856

Quality is also affected by the absence of a link between teachers' professional development to performance. The main programme which encourages and rewards teachers' professional development is the *Carrera Magisterial*, which was created in 1992 as part of an education reform. It is managed jointly by the Ministry of Education and the teachers' union. Most of the teachers can apply for training and about a third are enrolled (INEE, 2005). The scheme provides salary adjustments based on teachers scores on six criteria, including teacher and student performance, seniority and participation in training courses. In practice, the scheme is closer to a salary schedule than an incentive programme. Its design ensures that teachers that have enough years of seniority and regularly attend training courses, but who get average scores on evaluations, are promoted (Santibañez *et al.*, 2007). The teacher and student tests also focus more on knowledge of facts than on cognitive abilities, and the evaluation of teaching competencies is generally carried out by teachers from the same school instead of external evaluators, reducing reliability. Furthermore, once admission or promotion has been granted, the salary bonus remains effective for the rest of the teacher's professional life. This lack of incentives to improve performance has resulted in a weak association between student performance and the *Carrera Magisterial* status. Santibañez *et al.* (2007), for instance, detect only a modest improvement in student performance for teachers who are applying for *Carrera Magisterial* admission and no effect after the salary adjustment has been granted.

The low degree of school autonomy in Mexico compared to other OECD countries is another factor that can explain poor outcomes. School autonomy on budget allocations within schools, organisation of instruction, its content and personnel decisions are generally found to be positively related to student performance (Wößmann, 2007). In Mexico, decisions are generally taken at the central government or state level. While there are some policy initiatives that promote school autonomy, such as the quality school programme, these tend to be limited in school coverage and scope. The quality school programme, for instance, only covers around 20% of schools. While the programme grants schools considerable autonomy in budget allocations, this does not extend to the organisation of instruction, its content or personnel management. The choice of textbooks, instruction time and teaching methods, and decisions about hiring and firing of teachers remain outside the purview of school principals. Moving towards international best practice would require a broader reform which would grant schools more autonomy in areas identified as improving school performance.

Autonomy needs to be complemented by nation-wide exit exams to be effective (Wößmann, 2007). For instance, autonomy of schools to set teachers' salaries has been found to have a negative effect on student performance if it is accompanied by nation-wide exit examinations. This result may reflect opportunistic behaviour by school principals. Without exit examinations bad performance is not sanctioned, and school principals can set salaries in a way that promotes their own interests but not necessarily student performance. In Mexico there are no nation-wide exit examinations after lower secondary education (OECD, 2008b).

School autonomy is likely to boost performance most when linked to effective evaluation. Apart from setting nation-wide standards through central exit examinations, better outcomes can be achieved through evaluation and public posting of results (OECD, 2007a) that tend to promote parental and government pressure for quality. Schools in Mexico are evaluated on a regular basis through several evaluation tools (ENLACE, EXCALE, *Carrera Magisterial* tests among others) and the results are distributed to parents, teachers and school principals.[22] However, these assessment tools mainly test rote knowledge rather than analytical capabilities, and do not adjust for socioeconomic background. Therefore they do not assess school "value added", as distinct from the socioeconomic composition of students. Other OECD countries have introduced longitudinal testing to address this issue (OECD, 2008c). Finally, evaluation results do not explicitly trigger government actions. For instance, schools repeatedly performing poorly on the evaluations face no sanctions nor do they have to propose a restructuring plan to improve performance.

Some types of schools have particularly poor outcomes, pushing down average PISA scores (Figure 3.19). There are large differences between *Telesecundaria* that provides lower secondary education with television support and the "regular" schools. While this is partly explained by the weak socioeconomic background of students attending the *Telesecundaria*, as measured by the PISA index of economic, social and cultural status (ESCS), there may be quality issues as well. While *Telesecundaria* has been a cost effective tool to increase participation rates in the past – its target students had had little access to schools previously – the main challenge is now to ensure that students learn more when attending

Figure 3.19. **PISA score by secondary schools**

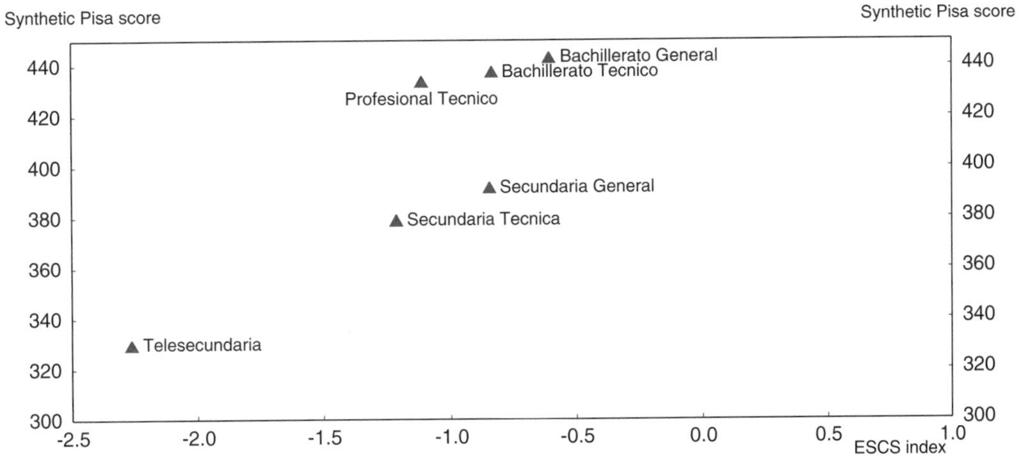

Source: INEE, PISA en México.

StatLink 📊 http://dx.doi.org/10.1787/684511887770

this type of school. There are also large differences between "regular" lower secondary schools (*Secundaria General, Secundaria Técnica*) and the upper secondary schools (*Profesional Tecnico, Bachillerato Tecnico, Bachillerato General*), which do not appear to be explained by socioeconomic background.[23] Instead, they may reflect both quality issues and the selection of better performing students into higher secondary education. To determine the part due to quality, the government should consider a careful evaluation of the various types of secondary schools.

There are also large differences in PISA outcomes between public and private schools – more than 40 points in the three PISA subject areas. These are likely to be explained by differences in socioeconomic background. Although INEE (2007b) does not report the ESCS index by school ownership, it notes that differences between public and private schools vanish at the upper secondary level. This can reflect the fact that only the better performing students in public lower-secondary schools are selected into public upper secondary schools, or that enrolment in private schools is higher at the upper secondary level, with a higher intake of students from weaker socioeconomic backgrounds.[24] Settling this issue would require further evaluation. Determining whether performance is explained by quality issues or socioeconomic background would help identify "best practices" and possible avenues for reform of the lower performing school types.

Competition between schools does not seem to be a barrier to better performance in Mexico. OECD (2007a) finds that countries with competition between schools achieve higher scores in the PISA science tests. According to principals' answers in the PISA 2006 evaluation, 84% of students in Mexico are enrolled in schools which are subject to competition from at least one other school, which is higher than the OECD average of 74%.

Education reforms

Mexico is addressing performance issues with reforms. A number of programmes aim to allocate more spending to non-wage items. *Enciclomedia* digitalises the school curriculum on CD-ROMs and makes the necessary computer equipment available to the participating schools to help students learn interactively with the aid of computers.[25] In 2006-07, the programme covered 150 000 fifth and sixth grade classrooms with a budget of around 1 500 million pesos (around 0.4% of total public education expenditure). Evaluations of the programme have generally been positive, but point out that more emphasis should be put on training teachers and providing basic infrastructure (electricity, appropriate classrooms, desks, etc.) as a precondition for using the relatively sophisticated computer equipment in the programme (Reimers, 2006). The quality school programme provides basic infrastructure to disadvantaged schools, which, however, must develop and implement a school restructuring plan (see Box 3.6). Finally, the Ministry of education has put in place several compensatory programmes, mostly financed through loans from the World Bank, that aim to improve school infrastructure, teaching material, teachers' and principals' incentives under the umbrella of CONAFE (National Council for Education Promotion). They cost about 200-300 million pesos (less than 0.1% of total public education spending per school year) (Santibañez et al., 2005).[26]

Box 3.6. **The Quality school programme**

The *Programa Escuelas de Calidad* (PEC), or quality school program aims at re-balancing the allocation of spending between wage and non-wage items. Although every Mexican primary and secondary school can participate, the PEC targets disadvantaged schools through direct mail, radio and other media. Participating schools receive five-year grants of up to 50 000 pesos (around 4 000 USD) per school year which are topped up by one additional peso for every peso raised by the school community (up to a ceiling of 50 000 pesos) in return for developing and implementing a re-structuring plan. This plan is jointly developed and implemented by the school community – teachers, parents, students and school administrators – and includes formal training for school principals. In the first four years schools must spend 80 per cent of the grant on supplies, infrastructure, and other non-wage items. In the fifth year, much of the spending goes to teacher training and development.

The programme started in 2001 in around 2 200 schools and had reached 38 000 schools in 2006-2007 (around 20% of all primary and secondary schools). Its relatively low budget (around 1 400 million pesos or 100 million US$) and the positive outcomes and feedback it has provided have turned the PEC into one of the Ministry's most praised programmes. Overall, formal evaluations by various organisations give it positive ratings (posted on the programme's website at *http://basica.sep.gob.mx/pec/*. A World Bank study, for instance, finds that the PEC decreases dropout and failure rates by 0.24 percentage points and repetition rates by 0.31 percentage points (Skoufias and Shapiro, 2006).

Another recent initiative, The *Alianza* for quality education (Box 3.7) aims to base teacher selection on national tests, improving school infrastructure and introducing performance incentives for teachers. While it addresses important weaknesses in the system, its voluntary nature may reduce effectiveness. In some states, the teachers' union has already refused to adopt it, and teachers have been striking against the tests.

Alianza aims at basing professional development on student performance, scores on teacher training programmes, and teacher performance. It is a welcome step towards improving teacher quality. This would improve on the "double counting" of seniority and highest academic degree in base salaries and the *Carrera Magisterial (CM)*. Nevertheless, a

---

Box 3.7. **Alliance for Quality Education**

In May 2008 President Calderón announced a voluntary agreement between the government and the 1.5 million member teachers' union (*Sindicato Nacional de los Trabajadores de la Educación*, SNTE) to improve the quality of education in Mexico, in the *Alianza por la Calidad de la Educación*.

Objective: Improve quality of education in Mexico.

Instruments:

- School modernisation: Infrastructure improvements; upgrading of information technology, creation of participatory school councils.

- Teacher professionalisation: Selection through independent agency; training and certification; improve incentives through reform of *Carrera Magisterial* and a new scheme exclusively based on student performance (*Programa de Estímulos a la Calidad Docente*).

- Improvement of student welfare: Improve health status (diet, lifestyle) and access (additional *Oportunidades* grants).

- Reform of curricula: Align with personal and professional needs.

- Evaluation: Evaluate all actors in the system (principals, teachers, students) and make them accountable.

The World Bank has signaled its support for the *Alianza* by committing to produce a yearly report on education in Mexico and to assist the government in its implementation. The *Alianza* addresses several of the main weaknesses of the Mexican education system. However, its implementation is facing resistance from some teachers. For instance, in the federal state Morelos a strike of the Morelos Section of the SNTE (Section 19) and the *Movimiento Magisterial de Base* has obliged the government to negotiate a separate agreement, mainly due to teachers' resistance against centralized entry exams for teachers. According to the newspaper El *Universal*, currently a large share of teachers' positions in Morelos are inherited.

---

more ambitious reform appears necessary to get the most out of *Carrera Magisterial*. Teacher and student tests should be reviewed and stronger emphasis put on cognitive abilities. There should be clear standards on the peer review of teacher performance, which should be carried out by external evaluators, possibly teachers who have reached the highest achievement level in the reformed *Carrera Magisterial*. Instead of granting salary bonuses for the rest of the career, there should be longitudinal testing of teachers. In this testing scheme teachers are evaluated repeatedly over time, and the test results of students are taken into account (OECD, 2008c). This would give teachers stronger incentives to continually improve their professional competencies and compensate for the initial disadvantage of teachers with students from weak socioeconomic backgrounds.[27]

The Oportunidades program aims to increase secondary enrolment rates. This cash transfer programme pays grants to low-income households conditional on regular school attendance and medical visits by children. It has been shown to boost school attendance rates, in particular of girls (Todd and Wolpin, 2006, Schultz, 2004). While this has increased enrolment rates in primary and lower secondary education to levels close to the OECD average, secondary school enrolment at age 15 remains low, especially among low-income groups (Figure 3.20).[28] To improve coverage from age 15 onwards, the government has recently introduced the *Jóvenes con Oportunidades* programme which gives cash-grants

Figure 3.20. **Secondary enrolment rate by income decile**
2006

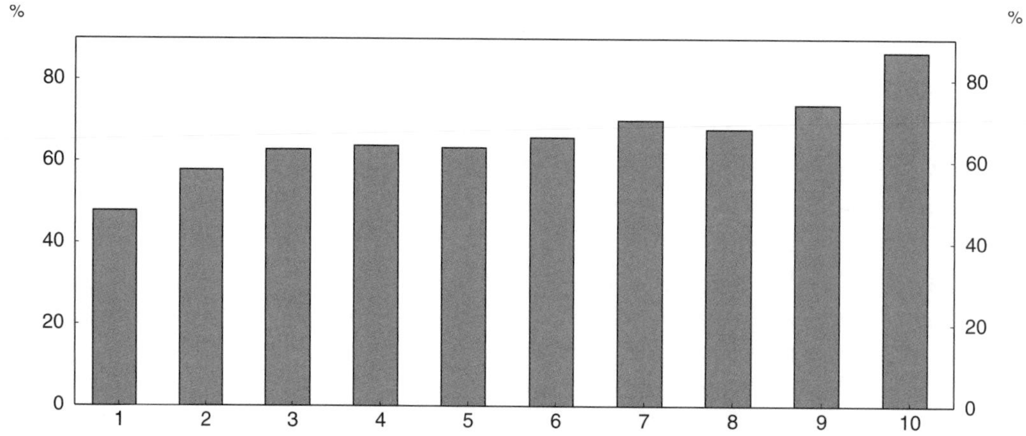

Source: ENIGH Household Income Survey 2006.

StatLink ⟋⟍ *http://dx.doi.org/10.1787/684558837868*

conditional upon secondary school completion. Increasing the scope of this program can be an efficient way to increase coverage. The efficiency of the programme should be evaluated continually, in particular to determine the optimal level of the grant.

What can be done to improve the efficiency of the education system?

The main challenges of the Mexican education system are to enhance performance incentives for schools and teachers, increase lower-secondary completion rates and enrolment in upper-secondary education. Weak incentives have contributed to low performance on the standardised PISA tests in which Mexico scores well below other OECD countries and its emerging market peers. Until recently the teacher selection process was non-transparent and the main professional development scheme puts excessive weight on seniority instead of teacher performance. Schools have limited autonomy in budgeting, instruction and personnel and there is no national exit exam after secondary education that would increase accountability to the government and parents. Existing evaluation schemes are fragmented and focus on knowledge instead of cognitive abilities. The *Alianza* for quality education addresses some of these issues but more needs to be done.

The teaching quality of newly hired teachers can be improved by basing teacher selection on the national teacher entry examination, as planned by the *Alianza* and implemented for the first time in 2008. Incentives for existing teachers can be raised by introducing voluntary re-certification and turning the *Carrera Magisterial* into a fully fledged incentive scheme, with a strong focus on student results and teaching performance. The reform of the *Carrera Magisterial* planned by the *Alianza* is welcome but the authorities should ensure that the evaluation of student results appropriately takes into account initial disadvantages related to weak socio economic backgrounds, either through regression analysis or through longitudinal testing. The peer review of teaching performance should be carried out by an independent panel.

Performance can also be improved by making schools more autonomous in budgeting, organisation, content of instruction, and in personnel decisions. This should be accompanied by steps to make schools more accountable to parents and the government through a national exit exam after lower secondary education. Consolidating the existing patchwork of evaluation schemes should also improve accountability of schools. Given that a national curriculum is in place, the authorities should focus on creating a single, comprehensive evaluation system that focuses strongly on cognitive abilities.

Low scores on the standardised PISA test are also related to the strong bias of education spending in favour of wages and against non-wage spending. New funds should mainly be allocated to the improvement of school infrastructure and educational material, and to the training of teachers. This could be achieved by expanding the existing *Enciclomedia* and Quality School Programmes that have received positive evaluations but currently only account for a small fraction of total education spending. The *Telesecundaria* programme, which has contributed to increases in secondary school coverage in remote rural areas in the past, should be evaluated to assess whether low performance is attributable to operation in disadvantaged areas or to quality issues.

To increase secondary school coverage the *Jóvenes con Oportunidades* programme should be expanded. Efficiency requires continual evaluation to make sure the level of the grant balances the objectives of increased coverage and low fiscal costs.

Concluding remarks

The recent government initiatives to reform the health and education systems go in the right directions. In health, substantial progress has been made in enrolling families that were previously not covered by existing insurance schemes. The over arching objective of health policy should be to achieve universal health insurance coverage, as well as to better integrate the existing insurer-provider networks. In education, the *Alianza* initiative includes some very promising measures for teachers and schools. The authorities should seize the opportunity to provide all children with a high-quality basic education. Box 3.8 provides a list of measures in health and education that would help to reach these goals.

Box 3.8. Main recommendations on increasing efficiency of spending on health and education

In health, the main challenges are to achieve universal health insurance coverage and reduce the fragmentation of the system.

- Continue efforts to achieve universal health insurance coverage through *Seguro Popular*. In particular, start discussions about making health insurance mandatory to avoid that adverse selection of less healthy individuals into *Seguro Popular* undermines its fiscal sustainability.

- Introduce a clear split between the functions of insurer and provider of care. Allow all insurers to contract with any provider. Establish a unified claims management system to reduce administrative costs.

- Set up a centralised roster of enrollees to reduce overlap between insurers and to improve the targeting of *Seguro Popular*.

In education, the main challenges are to improve teaching quality and to increase coverage of lower secondary education.

- Implement the national teacher entry examination to improve the professional qualification of newly hired teachers and introduce voluntary re-certification for existing teachers.

Box 3.8. **Main recommendations on increasing efficiency of spending on health and education** (cont.)

● Turn the *Carrera Magisterial* into a fully-fledged incentive scheme, with a strong focus on teaching performance.

● Make schools more autonomous in budget and personnel decisions.

● Accompany increased autonomy with measures to increase accountability, including by the introduction of a national exit exam after lower secondary education.

● Consolidate the existing patchwork of evaluation schemes.

● Channel new funds mainly to the improvement of school infrastructure, educational material and teacher training.

● Improve lower-secondary completion rates and enrolment in upper-secondary education by expanding the *Jóvenes con Oportunidades* programme.

Notes

1. OECD (2007a) identifies 38 points on the PISA science scale as the average difference between two students in successive grades.

2. Public social spending in Mexico, defined as the Social Development (Desarrollo Social) budget category, accounted for around 44% of total government spending and around 69% of programmable spending in 2006. The main item within this budget category is social security (9% of total), consisting mainly of retirement pensions, which is left out of the present study as it is not directly related to outcomes.

3. Using Ministry of Health (MoH) definition of covered population. See OECD (2005, p. 32) for a discussion of different definitions. *Source:* MoH submission.

4. At over 50% of total health expenditure, Mexico had the highest share of out-of-pocket payments in the OECD in 2005 (OECD, 2008a). This may be partly due to the poor availability of pharmaceutical drugs in the federal and state health services, obliging the uninsured population to purchase drugs in private pharmacies.

5. Social security contributions are fully deductible from income taxes, both for employers and employees. Social security contributions are split between i) a federal contribution equal to 13.9% of the inflation adjusted minimum wage in the federal district in 1997, ii) a flat employer contribution equal to 20.4% of the minimum wage, and iii) an income related contribution equal to 1.5% of workers' wages above three times the minimum wage. While employees earning less than three times the minimum wage are exempt from social security contributions, employers always pay the flat rate contribution.

6. Turkey has passed legislation on mandatory universal health insurance in 2008.

7. The difference in coverage of Seguro Popular in the MoH calculations in Table 3.1 and Figure 3.6 is mainly due to the strong growth in affiliation of SP between 2006 and 2008.

8. In systems without an insurer-provider split, there is generally only one vertically integrated insurer-provider to keep administration costs in check. This type of system is in place in the Nordic countries, Australia, Italy, Greece and Portugal, for instance.

9. An exception are IMSS hospitals. However, only spending on material inputs, which correspond to less than 10% of total spending, is financed through prospective payment arrangements.

10. IMSS-Oportunidades does not have a roster of covered individuals which would preclude this type of targeting errors.

11. The 2004 reform aims at increasing health care funds available to poorer states by providing additional federal funds through a subsidy to the states for every family affiliated to SP (Social Quota, SQ). Additionally, the federal transfer may be topped up by a Federal Solidarity Contribution (FSC) that takes into account, among others, the health risks and needs of the federal states. The SQ and the FSC are progressive, in the sense that new federal funds are mostly channeled to the poorer federal states. Moreover, federal states are required to contribute a minimum amount per

---

affiliated family from own resources to health care (State Solidarity Fund). Since richer states, in general, already contribute more to health care than the required amount, this increases public spending on health care mostly in the poorer federal states.

12. The results are obtained from a state-level regression of health spending per capita on GDP per capita. All variables are mean-differenced to purge the data from differences in average GDP per capita levels and average health spending per capita.

13. According to the MoH, by the end of 2008 the SP was covering around 27 million Mexicans.

14. Figures differ across surveys used for the evaluation. According to the SP impact survey (Encuesta de Impacto del Seguro Popular), the difference between the two groups is 2.2 percentage points, but only 3.5 according to the National Survey of Health and Nutrition (ENSANUT). The National Survey of Household Income and Expenditure (ENIGH) shows no significant difference between the two groups. While the study controls for individual characteristics of SP enrollees and the uninsured, and attempts at correcting for self-selection into SP, there are not enough details to judge the validity of the statistical procedures and results.

15. Auditoría (2007) expects the deficit to increase to 84 billion pesos by 2010, with the ratio of income to costs remaining at around 60%.

16. Formal employment is defined as salaried employment with registration at IMSS. Informal employment is defined as legal non-salaried employment (self-employment and workers remunerated through commissions) and illegal salaried employment, in the sense that employees receive a salary but are not registered with IMSS. Comisionistas are remunerated through commissions but do not receive a salary. In contrast to self-employed workers they do not own any productive assets and work for a firm.

17. Social security is explicitly subsidised through a federal transfer and implicitly subsidised through the deductibility of social security contributions from income taxes.

18. There has been an improvement since the PISA 2003 evaluation, in which Mexico scored at 399 points on the reading scale.

19. PISA 2006 classifies students into six proficiency levels in the three subject areas (five for reading). Students below level 2 are only able to solve straightforward and familiar problems. According to OECD (2007a), students who score below level 2 on the science scale, for instance, do not "demonstrate the science competencies that will enable them to participate effectively and productively in life situations related to science and technology." In the three PISA subject areas around 50% of students score below level 2 against an OECD average of around 20%, 47% on the reading scale (OECD average: 20.1%), 56.5% on the mathematics scale (21.3%), 51% on the science scale (19.3%).

20. Note that Simar and Wilson (2007) argue that the second-stage regression of DEA efficiency scores on environmental variables results in biased estimates. The size of the coefficient in the second-stage regression of DEA efficiency scores on the share of non-wage spending in total spending should therefore be interpreted with caution. However, plotting efficiency scores against the share of non-wage spending in total spending reveals that the most efficient countries are generally those with the highest share of non-wage spending.

21. The absence of centralised entry exams suggests that other determinants of teachers' professional qualifications, such as teaching competencies, also vary widely across federal states. A survey of the empirical evidence (Hanushek and Rivkin, 2006) concludes that these other determinants of teachers' qualifications tend to be more important than teachers' academic background.

22. According to a government submission.

23. The Secundaria para Trabajadores and Capacitación para el Trabajo have been excluded from the analysis as according to INEE (2007) the sample size is too low for these schools to allow statistical inference.

24. According to SEP (2008), 7.6% of lower secondary students are enrolled in private schools against 19.2% of upper secondary students.

25. It also makes the Encarta software, an electronic encyclopedia developed by Microsoft, available to the participating schools.

26. There is also an efficiency issue with regards to the allocation of spending between pre-school and primary/secondary education. The government is currently expanding pre-school education which, on the one hand, may divert resources from primary and secondary education. On the

other hand, pre-school education is generally found to improve educational achievement later in life.

27. These reforms would possibly lead to a higher satisfaction rate with CM. According to INEE (2005) around one third of teachers expressed in 2003 that CM was either not contributing or contributing litte to professional development.

28. Following OECD (2008b) secondary school enrolment rates are calculated as the share of children at between age 15 and 16 who are enrolled in secondary school.

Bibliography

Aaronson, D., L. Barrow and W. Sander (2007), "Teachers and student achievement in the Chicago public high schools", *Journal of Labor Economics* 25: 95-135.

Auditoría Superior de la Federación (2007), *Informe del Resultado de la Revisión y Fiscalizción Superior de la Cuenta Pública 2005*, Mexico.

CONAVI (2006), *Necesidades de Vivienda*, Comisión Nacional de Vivienda, Mexico.

Docteur, E. and H. Oxley (2003), "Health care systems: Lessons from the reform experience", OECD Economics Department Working Papers No. 4, OECD, Paris.

Frenk, J., E. Gonzalez-Pier, O. Gomez-Dantes, M. Lezana, F. Knaul (2006), "Comprehensive reform to improve health system performance in Mexico", *The Lancet* 368: 1524-1534.

ECLAC (2009), CEPALSTAT, *Latin American and Caribbean Statistics*, Economic Commission for Latin America and the Caribbean, Santiago.

Gakidou, E., R. Lozano, E. González-Pier, J. Abbott-Klafter, J. Barofsky, C. Bryson-Cahn, D. Feehan, D. Lee, H. Hernández-Llamas, C. Murray, "Assessing the effect of the 2001-2006 Mexican health reform: an interim report card", *The Lancet* 368: 1920-35.

Garber, A.M. and J. Skinner (2008), *Is American health care uniquely inefficient?*, NBER Working Paper 14257.

Gruen, R. and A. Howarth (2005), "Financial Management in Health Services", McGraw-Hill, New York.

Guichard, S. (2005), "The education challenge in Mexico", Economics Department Working Paper No. 447, OECD, Paris.

Hadley, J. (2003), "Sick and poorer – the consequences of being uninsured: A review of the research on the relationship between health insurance, medical care use, health, work, and income", *Medical Care Research and Review* 60(2) (Supplement to June 2003): 3S-75S.

Hanushek, E. (2008), "Incentives for efficiency and equity in the school system", *Perspektiven der Wirtschaftspolitik* 9 (Special Issue): 5-27.

IMSS (2008), *Informe al Ejecutivo Federal y al Congreso de la Unión sobre la Situación Financiera y los Riesgos del Instituto Mexicano del Seguro Social*, Mexico City.

INEE (2005), *Panorama Educativo de México 2005*, Instituto Nacional para la Evaluación de la Educación, Mexico.

INEE (2007a), *Panorama Educativo de México 2007*, Instituto Nacional para la Evaluación de la Educación, Mexico.

INEE (2007b), *PISA 2006 en México*, Instituto Nacionál para la Evaluación de la Educación, Mexico.

INEE (2008), *Panorama Educativo de México 2008*, Instituto Nacional para la Evaluación de la Educación, Mexico.

INS (2008), *Sistema de Protección Social en Salud. Evaluación de Procesos Administrativos*, Instituto Nacional de Salud Pública.

Joumard, I. (2005), "Getting the most out of public sector decentralisation in Mexico", Economics Working Paper No. 453, OECD, Paris.

Joumard, I., C. André, C. Nicq and O. Chatal (2008), "Health status determinants: lifestyle, environment, health care resources and efficiency", Economics Working Paper No. 627, OECD, Paris.

Levy, S. (2008), "Good Intentions, Bad Outcomes: Social Policy, Informality, and Economic Growth in Mexico", Brookings Institution Press, Washington DC.

Nigenda, G., J. Ruíz, Y. Rosales, R. Berejano (2006), "Enfermeras con licenciatura en México: estimación de los niveles de deserción escolar y desperdicio laboral", *Salud Pública de México* 48(1): 22-29.

OECD (2004), *Learning for Tomorrow's World: First Results from PISA 2003*, OECD, Paris.

OECD (2005), *Reviews of Health Systems: Mexico*, OECD, Paris.

OECD (2007a), *PISA 2006. Vol. 1: Analysis*, OECD, Paris.

OECD (2007b), *PISA 2006. Vol. 2: Data*, OECD, Paris.

OECD (2008a), Health Data, OECD, Paris.

OECD (2008b), *Education at a Glance: OECD Indicators*, OECD, Paris.

OECD (2008c), *Measuring Improvements in Learning Outcomes – Best Practices to Assess the Value Added of Schools*, OECD, Paris.

OECD (2009), *Reviews of Health Systems: Turkey*, OECD, Paris (forthcoming).

Reimers (2006) (ed.), Aprender *más y mejor. Políticas, programas y oportunidades de aprendizaje en educación básica en México*, Fondo de Cúltura Económica, Mexico.

Rivkin, S., E. Hanushek and J. Kain (2005), "Teachers, schools, and academic achievement", *Econometrica* 73: 417-458.

Santibañez, L., G. Vernez, P. Razquin (2005), Education in Mexico Challenges and Opportunities, RAND Documented Briefing, Santa Monica, CA.

Santibañez, L., J.F. Martínez, A. Datar, P.J. McEwan, C. Messan Setodji, R. Basurta-Dávila (2007), Breaking ground: Analysis of the assessment system and impact of Mexico's teacher incentive program Carrera Magisterial', *RAND Technical Report*, Santa Monica, CA.

Schultz, P. (2004), "School subsidies for the poor: Evaluating the Mexican Progresa poverty program", *Journal of Development Economics* 74: 199-250.

SEP (2007), *Sistema Educativo de los Estados Unidos Méxicanos. Principales Cifras. Ciclo Escolár 2007-2008*, Secretaría de Educación Pública, Mexico.

Simar, L. and P. Wilson (1998), "Sensitivity analysis of efficiency scores: How to bootstrap in nonparametric frontier models", *Management Science* 44: 49-61.

Simar, L. and P. Wilson (2000), "Statistical inference in nonparametric frontier models: The state of the art", *Journal of Productivity Analysis* 13: 49-78.

Simar, L. and P. Wilson (2007), "Estimation and inference in two-stage, semi-parametric models of production processes", *Journal of Econometrics* 136: 31-64.

Skoufias, E. and J. Shapiro (2006), "Evaluating the Impact of Mexico's Quality Schools Program:The Pitfalls of Using Nonexperimental Data", *World Bank Policy Research Paper* 4036, World Bank, Washington DC.

Sutherland, D., I. Joumard and C. Nicq (2007), "Performance indicators for public spending efficiency in primary and secondary education", *Economics Working Paper* No. 546, OECD, Paris.

Todd, P. and K Wolpin (2006), "Assessing the impact of a school subsidy programme in Mexico: Using a social experiment to validate a dynamic behavioural model of child schooling and fertility", *American Economic Review* 96: 1384-1417.

WHO (2007), *World Health Statistics 2007*, World Health Organization, Geneva.

Wößmann, L. (2007), "International evidence on school competition, autonomy, and accountability: A review", *Peabody Journal of Education* 82(2-3): 473-497.

World Bank (2004), "Universal Health Insurance Coverage in Mexico: In Search of Alternatives", World Bank, Washington DC.

World Bank (2005), "Income Generation and Social Protection for the Poor", World Bank, Washington DC.

ANNEX 3.A1

Details on data envelopment analysis (DEA)

Health

DEA efficiency scores for health spending are calculated using life expectancy as a proxy of health system outcomes. Life expectancy at birth has the advantage of being a very broad measure of the population's health status, summarising status in a multitude of health areas, but has the drawback that it is influenced by factors not directly related to the health care system. On the input side it is accounted for one input and two environmental variables. Total health spending per capita measures the resources spent on health care, both private and public. GDP per capita measures the income level of the population and can be thought of as summarising a broad variety of influences on the population's health status. Fruits and vegetables consumption proxies the population's way of life which may also have an influence on its health status. The reference year for the outcome and input variables is the year 2005. To test the robustness of the obtained results estimations have been repeated replacing GDP per capita by the PISA index of economic, social and cultural status (ESCS), which summarises occupational, educational and cultural attainment of the population. Results obtained using the ESCS index are similar to the ones reported here. The estimation sample includes 29 OECD and 15 emerging countries with GDP per capita above 8 000 PPP USD for which all outcome, input and environmental variables are available. The reported efficiency scores are corrected for small sample bias using the procedure proposed by Simar and Wilson (1998, 2000). This procedure accounts for the fact that due to the small sample of countries the efficient country is likely to be omitted, which would bias the efficiency scores upward. Moreover, it provides confidence intervals around the obtained efficiency scores. Due to the small sample correction procedure no country is found to be on the efficiency frontier. The detailed DEA results including observed values of the outcome and input variables, confidence intervals and potential efficiency gains are reported in Tables 3.A1.1 and 3.A1.2. The reported results are obtained under the assumption of non-increasing returns to scale in production.

Education

Efficiency scores for the Mexican education system are calculated using as the outcome variable a synthetic PISA score that combines the reading, mathematics and science scores of the 2006 evaluation through factor analysis. The input variables are education spending per student and the PISA ESCS index as an environmental variable. Education spending per student is measured as the average of spending per secondary student in PPP USD over the 2000-2007 period. It would be preferable to use a measure of

Table 3.A1.1. **Life expectancy at birth as outcome variable**

Country	Life expectancy at birth	Total health spending	GDP/capita	Fruits and vegetables consumption	Output efficiency score	95% confidence interval	Potential increase in life expectancy
ARG	74.8	1 107	10 815	1.50	0.956	[0.938, 0.971]	3.41
AUS	80.8	3 000	31 656	1.96	0.978	[0.968, 0.984]	1.81
AUT	79.4	3 487	34 075	2.27	0.963	[0.956, 0.967]	3.02
BEL	79.5	3 088	31 699	1.98	0.962	[0.952, 0.968]	3.13
BGR	72.6	722	9 328	1.89	0.944	[0.926, 0.959]	4.30
BRA	71.8	666	8 474	1.35	0.971	[0.941, 0.999]	2.11
CAN	80.2	3 425	34 972	2.39	0.973	[0.966, 0.977]	2.19
CHE	81.2	4 072	35 182	2.00	0.985	[0.976, 0.989]	1.24
CHL	78.2	666	12 173	1.57	0.969	[0.933, 0.999]	2.48
CZE	75.9	1 445	20 280	1.50	0.946	[0.934, 0.957]	4.32
DEU	78.9	3 269	30 445	2.03	0.954	[0.945, 0.961]	3.77
DNK	77.8	3 063	33 645	2.48	0.944	[0.937, 0.948]	4.60
ESP	80.6	2 254	27 180	2.55	0.982	[0.975, 0.989]	1.48
EST	72.6	831	16 677	1.73	0.915	[0.900, 0.924]	6.78
FIN	78.8	2 309	30 462	1.61	0.950	[0.932, 0.964]	4.15
FRA	80.2	3 329	30 591	2.37	0.971	[0.964, 0.977]	2.36
GBR	78.9	2 597	31 371	2.06	0.953	[0.944, 0.961]	3.92
GRC	79.0	2 954	29 261	4.22	0.959	[0.953, 0.964]	3.34
HRV	75.2	985	13 231	1.98	0.950	[0.937, 0.959]	3.96
HUN	72.6	1 328	17 014	1.88	0.910	[0.901, 0.916]	7.16
IRL	79.4	3 139	37 887	2.19	0.963	[0.955, 0.967]	3.04
ISL	81.1	3 344	35 465	1.61	0.974	[0.952, 0.988]	2.18
ISR	79.7	1 850	22 886	3.36	0.984	[0.978, 0.990]	1.27
ITA	80.3	2 474	27 750	3.08	0.979	[0.973, 0.985]	1.71
JPN	82.1	2 498	30 290	1.58	0.980	[0.959, 0.999]	1.72
KOR	78.4	1 263	21 273	2.74	0.980	[0.970, 0.986]	1.61
LTU	71.3	837	14 084	1.68	0.896	[0.882, 0.907]	8.25
LVA	71.4	840	13 215	1.52	0.901	[0.885, 0.913]	7.84
MEX	**74.4**	**725**	**11 387**	**1.78**	**0.946**	[0.929, 0.960]	**4.26**
MNE	74.3	657	8 160	2.23	0.967	[0.920, 0.999]	2.54
NLD	79.3	3 187	34 492	2.55	0.963	[0.956, 0.967]	3.05
NOR	80.0	4 307	47 538	1.90	0.969	[0.959, 0.975]	2.53
NZL	79.7	2 223	24 566	2.44	0.981	[0.975, 0.986]	1.55
POL	75.0	843	13 571	1.47	0.952	[0.936, 0.964]	3.79
PRT	78.1	2 046	19 956	2.97	0.972	[0.965, 0.977]	2.21
ROM	71.7	513	9 368	2.43	0.981	[0.952, 0.999]	1.42
RUS	65.5	615	11 861	1.44	0.893	[0.867, 0.909]	7.88
SRB	72.6	520	8 644	2.23	0.969	[0.923, 0.999]	2.34
SVK	73.9	1 129	15 881	1.29	0.949	[0.920, 0.966]	4.00
SVN	77.6	1 959	23 010	2.14	0.958	[0.951, 0.963]	3.42
SWE	80.5	3 013	32 016	1.93	0.974	[0.964, 0.981]	2.13
TUR	71.3	593	10 370	3.37	0.928	[0.909, 0.945]	5.50
URY	75.6	745	9 266	1.25	0.967	[0.917, 0.999]	2.62
USA	77.7	6 350	41 813	2.36	0.944	[0.938, 0.947]	4.60

cumulative spending over a student's theoretical years of schooling but this data is only available for a subset of OECD countries. Results in terms of efficiency ranking are similar to the ones presented in the main text if this alternative measure of education spending is used. The estimation sample includes 28 OECD and 14 emerging countries with GDP per capita above 8 000 PPP USD for which all outcome, input and environmental variables are

Table 3.A1.2. **PISA scores as outcome variable**

Country	Synthetic PISA score	Spending per student (secondary)	ESCS	Output efficiency score	95% confidence interval	Potential increase in PISA score
ARG	382	1 591	−0.64	0.832	[0.785, 0.832]	90
AUS	520	4 301	0.21	0.967	[0.932, 0.967]	27
AUT	502	9 107	0.2	0.908	[0.887, 0.908]	56
BEL	510	8 043	0.17	0.923	[0.901, 0.923]	48
BGR	416	1 534	−0.21	0.913	[0.863, 0.913]	49
BRA	384	855	−1.12	0.997	[0.854, 0.997]	32
CHE	514	9 817	0.09	0.931	[0.909, 0.931]	43
CHL	430	1 640	−0.7	0.933	[0.878, 0.933]	44
CZE	502	3 966	0.03	0.944	[0.910, 0.944]	39
DEU	505	6 530	0.29	0.921	[0.900, 0.921]	49
DNK	501	11 543	0.31	0.905	[0.884, 0.905]	58
ESP	476	6 104	−0.31	0.875	[0.835, 0.875]	79
EST	516	3 427	0.14	0.987	[0.951, 0.987]	14
FIN	553	8 224	0.26	0.998	[0.974, 0.998]	7
FRA	493	8 440	−0.09	0.897	[0.869, 0.897]	64
GBR	502	7 621	0.19	0.909	[0.888, 0.909]	56
GRC	464	5 894	−0.15	0.851	[0.822, 0.851]	90
HKG	542	6 308	−0.67	0.997	[0.912, 0.997]	27
HRV	479	3 012	−0.11	0.929	[0.889, 0.929]	46
HUN	492	3 404	−0.09	0.943	[0.907, 0.943]	39
IRL	509	6 705	−0.02	0.928	[0.903, 0.928]	45
ISL	494	6 953	0.77	0.898	[0.878, 0.898]	61
ISR	445	5 079	0.22	0.818	[0.790, 0.818]	108
ITA	469	7 733	−0.07	0.852	[0.827, 0.852]	88
JPN	517	6 430	−0.01	0.945	[0.920, 0.945]	36
KOR	542	4 617	−0.01	0.997	[0.958, 0.997]	14
LTU	481	2 670	0.04	0.944	[0.897, 0.944]	39
LUX	485	15 652	0.09	0.880	[0.859, 0.880]	72
LVA	485	2 478	−0.02	0.968	[0.924, 0.968]	25
MAC	509	2 666	−0.91	0.998	[0.891, 0.998]	36
MEX	**409**	**1 833**	**−0.99**	**0.882**	**[0.812, 0.882]**	**74**
NLD	521	7 765	0.25	0.943	[0.921, 0.943]	37
NOR	487	13 343	0.42	0.880	[0.859, 0.880]	72
NZL	524	5 285	0.1	0.962	[0.932, 0.962]	29
POL	500	2 669	−0.3	0.981	[0.928, 0.981]	24
PRT	471	6 332	−0.62	0.867	[0.798, 0.867]	93
ROM	410	1 258	−0.37	0.924	[0.858, 0.924]	49
SVK	482	2 360	−0.15	0.973	[0.930, 0.973]	22
SVN	506	6 061	0.13	0.924	[0.901, 0.924]	47
SWE	504	8 762	0.24	0.911	[0.889, 0.911]	55
TUR	432	1 408	−1.28	0.997	[0.852, 0.997]	37
URY	423	844	−0.51	0.997	[0.864, 0.997]	35

available. The reported efficiency scores are corrected for small sample bias using the procedure proposed by Simar and Wilson (1998, 2000) and are obtained under the assumption of non-increasing returns to scale in production.

ISBN 978-92-64-05441-7
OECD Economic Surveys: Mexico
© OECD 2009

Chapter 4

Pedal to the metal: Structural reforms to boost long-term growth and spur recovery from the crisis

While Mexico's growth performance has gradually improved over the past decades, its convergence toward OECD countries has been less rapid than in several other emerging markets.The recent significant reductions in import tariffs should help the economy take fuller advantage of trade and investment integration, which could be a relative strength for Mexico given its geographic location. Reforms introduced in the past two years, including those to promote competition and transparency in the financial sector and, to a lesser extent in telecommunications, will also stimulate the dynamism of the economy. Despite this progress, further reforms are needed to boost overall and within-sector productivity. Relative weaknesses in education, infrastructure, financial development, the rule of law, as well as a lack of competition come out in various studies as explaining why Mexico has not grown as fast as other countries. Focusing attention now on reforms in areas with rapid pay-offs such as improving competitiveness and infrastructure could yield double benefits in supporting the recovery from the current recession and longer-term growth. This can be achieved by increasing competition, especially in network industries, liberalizing further the foreign investment and trade regimes, and improving education coverage and trade-related infrastructure.

Mexico's growth record has not been stellar over the past decades and, as a result, living standards are not converging towards the higher income levels enjoyed elsewhere. The historical experience of Japan, for example, suggests that the challenge of catching-up can be met and have far-reaching positive consequences. In 1950 Mexico and Japan had approximately the same level of GDP per capita. In the subsequent 40 years Mexico continued its relative decline vis-à-vis the United States contributing to the large gap in living standards between the two countries (Figure 4.1), while Japan enjoyed sustained growth and achieved one of the highest standards of living in the world. There have

Figure 4.1. **The sources of real GDP per capita differences, 2007**

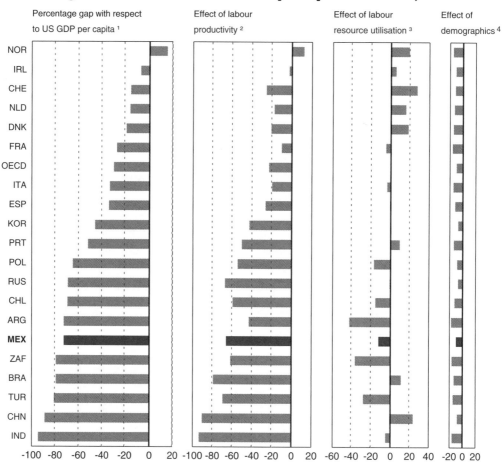

1. Based on 2005 purchasing power parities (PPPs).
2. Labour productivity is measured as GDP per person employed.
3. Labour resource utilisation is measured as the ratio of those employed to the persons of working age.
4. Measures the change in the ratio of persons of working age (15-64 years) to the total population.

Source: OECD, National Accounts; World Bank , WDI; International Monetary Fund, WEO; United Nations, UNSD.

StatLink ᘓ᠍ᘖ http://dx.doi.org/10.1787/684560726636

nonetheless been some improvements towards raising growth more recently in Mexico. Although growth of GDP per capita remains low compared to other dynamic emerging markets, it is now around 2% per annum, close to the OECD average and a vast improvement from stagnation in the late 1980s in the aftermath of the Latin American debt crisis. Instrumental to this have been reforms to open the economy to greater trade and investment and the establishment of macroeconomic stability. Implementing growth-friendly reforms would improve long-term prospects and could help in recovering from the crisis. In particular, measures such as competitively priced telecommunications services, adequate transport infrastructure, improving education outcomes and a more attractive climate for foreign investment would boost competitiveness and sustain demand. Greater competition would also contain price pressures and increase purchasing power over time.

This chapter discusses Mexico's growth performance and policy reforms to improve it. The first section compares the growth performance with that of other countries. In the second section, the sources of growth are examined with a view to identifying the causes of structural weaknesses (see Annex 4.A2 for data sources). The chapter ends by highlighting the structural policy areas that Mexico should address to shift to a higher growth path and sustain recovery and demand in both the short run and longer term.

Mexico's growth performance compared – some salient facts

Mexico's GDP growth has been low among emerging markets (Table 4.1).[1] Together with Brazil, South Africa and Russia (a special case however due to the collapse of the planned economy) Mexico grew at rates around or below those observed on average in the OECD over the past two decades. By contrast, the better-performing emerging markets – Chile, China, India and Turkey – have grown rapidly during the whole period ranging from about 4% on average for Turkey to a spectacular 10% for China. Looking at the two decades separately shows that, while higher-income countries recorded a slow-down in their activity between the sub-periods, all the emerging countries (except Chile) increased their real GDP growth rates.

Table 4.1. **Real GDP at 2005 prices and PPPs (US dollars)**

	In Millions		Annual average growth rates		
	1987	2007	1987-1997	1997-2007	1987-2007
United States	7 173 680	13 016 677	3.13	2.91	3.02
OECD average	705 788	1 198 673	2.74	2.62	2.68
Brazil	1 034 218	1 716 542	2.17	2.97	2.57
Chile	74 146	221 005	6.72	4.52	5.61
China	1 005 139	6 704 554	9.87	10.03	9.95
India	851 278	2 921 748	5.41	7.31	6.36
Mexico	**711 849**	**1 270 664**	**2.72**	**3.16**	**2.94**
Russian Federation	1 822 455	1 917 612	−5.03	4.74	0.28
S. Africa	259 056	436 754	1.52	3.78	2.65
Turkey	275 081	621 864	3.89	4.43	4.16

Source: OECD estimations. Where unavailable, World Bank (WDI), International Monetary Fund (WEO) and United Nations (UNSD).

Average GDP per capita growth rates over the last two decades are quite heterogeneous across the countries analyzed (Table 4.2). Over the past two decades, Mexico has grown more slowly than the United States, the OECD and the other emerging markets in the sample, except South Africa and Brazil (Table 4.2). This should have been a period of catch up. However, the trend over time is more encouraging – GDP growth increased from 0.7% in the first decade to 1.9% in the second and closer to the OECD average.

Table 4.2. **Real GDP per capita**

	In 2005 PPPs (US dollars)		Annual average growth rates		
	1987	2007	1987-1997	1997-2007	1987-2007
United States	29 553	43 026	1.95	1.84	1.90
OECD average	20 800	30 410	1.92	1.92	1.92
Brazil	7 474	9 072	0.45	1.50	0.97
Chile	5 942	13 323	5.06	3.19	4.12
China	918	5 052	8.56	9.24	8.90
India	1 098	2 587	3.26	5.50	4.38
Mexico	**9 250**	**11 983**	**0.70**	**1.91**	**1.30**
Russian Federation	10 199	13 482	−4.39	5.16	1.88
S. Africa	7 492	9 096	−0.53	2.50	0.97
Turkey	5 230	8 387	1.87	2.91	2.39

Source: OECD estimations. Where unavailable, World Bank (WDI), International Monetary Fund (WEO) and United Nations (UNSD).

Sources of differences in living standards and growth

A comparison of sources of growth among emerging markets shows that weaker labour productivity is the principal reason accounting for Mexico's relatively weak performance. Labour productivity growth was slightly negative over the past 20 years in Mexico, while it was the main driver of growth in the better performing economies (Figure 4.2).

Figure 4.2. **Sources of growth**
Average growth, 1987-2007

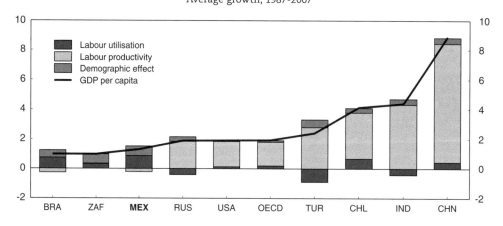

Source: OECD, National Accounts; World Bank, WDI; International Monetary Fund, WEO; United Nations, UNSD.

StatLink ᴍ╤ᴙ http://dx.doi.org/10.1787/684616077122

Breaking down Mexico's performance further into 5-year periods reveals a more encouraging story, as productivity growth has increased continuously from each 5-year period to the next. Per capita GDP trend growth has been close to the OECD average during the last 5-year period (around 2% per annum), although it remained well below that in better performing emerging markets. The accelerating labour productivity explains the increasing GDP per capita growth rate over time (Table 4.3).

Table 4.3. **Mexico: Sources of growth over time**

Mexico	1987-1992	1992-1997	1997-2002	2002-2007
GDP	2.44	2.99	3.16	3.16
GDP per capita	0.25	1.15	1.76	2.06
Labour Productivity	−2.03	−0.75	0.82	1.11
Labour Utilisation	1.73	1.32	0.24	0.21
Demographics	0.59	0.59	0.68	0.73

Source: OECD estimations. Where unavailable, World Bank (WDI) and International Monetary Fund (WEO) and United Nations.

Sectoral labour productivity and shift-share analysis

A breakdown by industry shows that the poor performance was broad based.[2] In Mexico, the weak relative performance of productivity applies to about 80% of total employment—in agriculture, manufacturing, wholesale and retail trade and government and social services (Figure 4.3a).[3] Even in the latest five-year period when Mexico's relative

Figure 4.3. **Trend sectoral labour productivity growth**

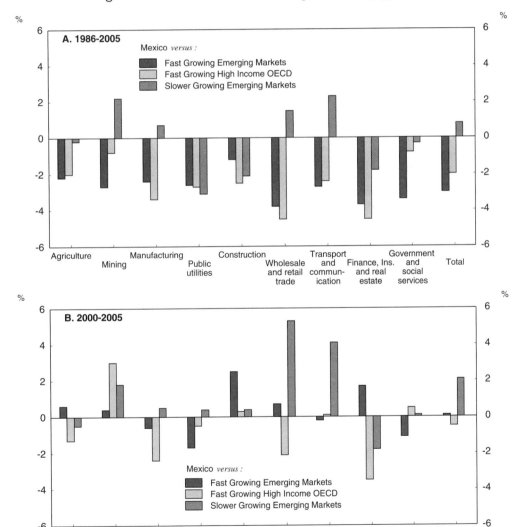

Source: OECD, based on EU KLEMS database; Groningen Growth and Development Center.

StatLink http://dx.doi.org/10.1787/684646082118

aggregate performance was strongest, it still had lower growth in agriculture, manufacturing, wholesale and retail trade than in the higher income OECD countries. Mexico had also not fully closed the growth gap in utilities and government and social services with the fast growing emerging markets (Figure 4.3b).

The total change in productivity can be further broken down into a "within-sector" effect (driven by technical change and capital accumulation), a "between-sector" effect (reallocation of labour resources between sectors), and a "cross-sector effect", that captures the interaction of productivity changes and employment shares. Between-sector effects dominated in Mexico until recently and accounted for the largest proportion of total labour productivity growth in the sample (Figure 4.4). This was mostly due to a large fall in agricultural employment, a sector with relatively low productivity. For the past 20 years within-sector productivity growth in Mexico was low compared to most other countries. Negative cross-sector effects also largely offset the positive between-sector effect and account for a higher proportion of total productivity change compared to other countries. This occurred because sectors with relatively poor productivity growth, such as wholesale and retail trade and construction, gained employment share.

Figure 4.4. **Shift-share analysis**
Percentage of the sum of absolute changes in the components

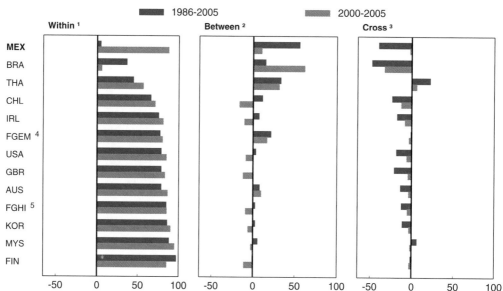

1. Within: within sector labour productivity.
2. Between: productivity growth due to reallocation of labour across sectors with different levels of productivity.
3. Cross: productivity growth from shifts of employment across sectors with different productivity growth rates.
4. FGEM for Fast Growing Emerging Markets.
5. FGHI for Fast Growing High Income OECD.
Source: OECD, based on EU KLEMS database.

StatLink ⟶ http://dx.doi.org/10.1787/684652282530

In more recent years, productivity growth in Mexico has been mainly driven by within-sector productivity, a pattern more similar to other countries. Between-sector effects had a much smaller role as the economy matured and the rate of decline of agriculture's share of total employment eased. Small negative cross-sector effects were also much more in line with other countries. This occurred because the productivity gap between growth in slow

OECD ECONOMIC SURVEYS: MEXICO – ISBN 978-92-64-05441-7 – © OECD 2009 growing Mexican sectors gaining employment share and fast growing sectors losing employment share (such as mining) closed.

The changing pattern suggests that Mexico's more recent sectoral pattern of productivity growth is becoming more similar to that of higher income countries. It is supported by productivity change at the industry level in contrast to the 1986-2000 period when productivity growth was mainly a product of labour migrating from agriculture to industry. Although labour productivity and GDP per capita growth rates have increased, they remain too low to allow rapid convergence with the high-income OECD countries. Within-sector productivity growth can be further boosted by capital, innovation and competition, which tend to be closely related to education, FDI and financial sector development.

Mexico's convergence with high-income countries has been slow

The slow pattern of Mexico's convergence towards higher-income levels is at odds with what is suggested by conventional economic theory. In principle, lower-income countries should grow faster than higher-income ones, due to diminishing returns to capital (Box 4.1). Empirically there is some evidence that this theory of convergence holds, but it is far from automatic (Figure 4.5). There are both converging and diverging countries

---

Box 4.1. **Growth models, convergence and policy**

Growth models tend to explain increases in output through the accumulation of inputs that make a contribution to the production process, and typically imply that public policy has a potentially strong role in influencing these processes.

A seminal model of economic growth, the augmented Solow-Swan model (Solow, 1956, 1957 and Swan, 1956), uses a neoclassical production function, $Y = F (K; AL)$ where the marginal productivity is positive but decreasing for both factors, capital (K) and labour (L). Technical progress, A, grows at an exogenous and constant rate and increases labour productivity. In this model, capital, labour and the economy move towards a long-run steady state where a constant growth rate is determined by the population and technical progress growth rates. During the transition, the speed of convergence will decrease as the economy approaches its steady state because of diminishing marginal returns to capital. Richer countries closer to the steady state will grow slower than poorer ones. This convergence will only be absolute, *i.e.* to the same level of income per capita, if all countries have the same steady state. This in turn will only occur if the parameters that determine the steady state, population growth and rate of technical progress, are identical across countries. As these factors and, in particular, technical progress (representing here everything that augments labour productivity) are neither exogenous nor constant across countries convergence to similar income levels is not automatic. Public policy can have a large influence on technical progress as defined in the model and therefore significantly affect the convergence rates of countries.

The role of public policy is even clearer in the endogenous growth models. The most famous ones are the two-sector AK – or the Uzawa-Lucas – model (Uzawa (1961), Lucas (1988)) and Romer's model (1990). In these models diminishing returns to factor accumulation do not necessarily arise, and convergence is no longer a property of the growth process. Growth is driven in the long-run by factors such as human capital and research and development, where public policy has a strong potential influence.

Figure 4.5. **Convergence towards the leader**

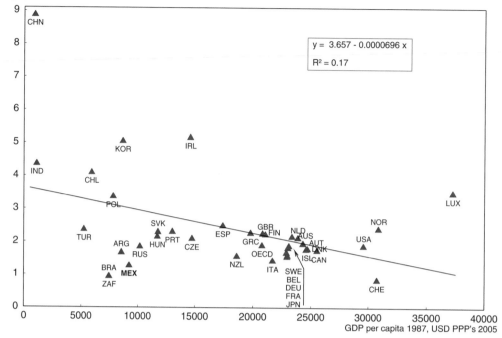

Source: OECD, National Accounts; World Bank, WDI; International Monetary Fund, WEO; United Nations, UNSD.

StatLink 🔗 http://dx.doi.org/10.1787/684703536423

within the OECD members and the selected emerging markets. However, the diversity of growth patterns between emerging countries is greater than for the high-income OECD economies, which tend to show more homogeneous growth paths.

The speed of convergence has also varied in history. The United States took a relatively short period of time to converge and surpass the 19th century leader, the United Kingdom. By contrast, Japan and Germany diverged from the leader prior to the mid 20th century and then converged rapidly after World War II, while Mexico continued to diverge (Figure 4.6).

Figure 4.6. **GDP per capita**
1990 USD PPP's

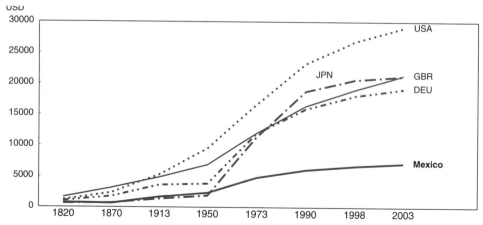

Source: Angus Madison (2003), The World Economy: Historical Statistics.

StatLink 🔗 http://dx.doi.org/10.1787/684703867804

OECD ECONOMIC SURVEYS: MEXICO – ISBN 978-92-64-05441-7 – © OECD 2009

The speed of convergence has reflected differences in policies, saving and population growth rates. The latter influence convergence as they determine the steady state countries are converging to. Higher policy variance is related to the rate of technical progress, which tends to be important in emerging markets. Indeed, the catch up process should be seen as a potential one that has to be stimulated through sound policies rather than one that will happen naturally. Historical evidence suggests that divergent performance can endure a long time, which underlines the importance of ensuring the right policy mix that will lift growth.

To further emphasize the importance of growth-enhancing reforms, the speed of convergence towards living standards in the United States under different growth scenarios is examined (Table 4.4). This shows that if the speed of convergence observed for the past two decades continued, several emerging markets in the sample, including Mexico, would diverge from the United States or converge only slowly. The situation improves notably for Mexico if the last decade (which benefited from macroeconomic and trade policy reforms) is extrapolated – the country switches from divergence to convergence, although convergence would still take a very long time. Economic reform that generates extra growth can have large effects. A 1% lift in Mexico's relative growth rate over the past decades would have moved Mexico from divergence to convergence at rates much faster than extrapolating even the 1997-2007 period.

Table 4.4. **Years to reach complete convergence with the United States**

	GDP per capita at 2005 PPPs (USD); (United States = 100)			Years to reach convergence		
	1987	1997	2007	I	II	III
Russian Federation	n/d	22.73	31.33	−6 511	36	121
Mexico	**31.30**	**27.66**	**27.85**	**−219**	**1 848**	**321**
Brazil	25.29	21.80	21.09	−171	−470	2029
South Africa	25.35	19.81	21.14	−171	239	2008
China	3.11	5.82	11.74	32	31	28
Chile	20.10	27.14	30.97	54	89	38
India	3.72	4.22	6.01	117	80	84
Turkey	17.70	17.55	19.49	338	156	112
OECD average	70.38	70.13	70.68	1 640	442	35

I. – Years to reach convergence (87-07 speed of convergence)
II. – Years to reach convergence (97-07 speed of convergence)
III. – Years to reach convergence (87-07 speed of convergence augmented by 1%)
Note: Negative numbers indicate a diverging process
Source: OECD estimates. Where unavailable, World Bank (WDI), International Monetary Fund (WEO) and United Nations (UNSD)

Growth in Mexico has relied more on the accumulation of production factors than on rising productivity. Over the past twenty years, Mexico's growth pattern has been "extensive" – i.e. based on the growth of labour utilisation and changes in demographic structure (Figure 4.7). By contrast, the better performing countries, such as Chile, China, India, and Turkey exhibit an "intensive" growth path, with a greater reliance on high labour productivity growth rates.

Again, breaking down performance over time reveals a more positive story. Mexico's growth pattern has become more technology intensive. While labour productivity has been

Figure 4.7. **GDP per capita, various convergence patterns**
USA 2007 = 100

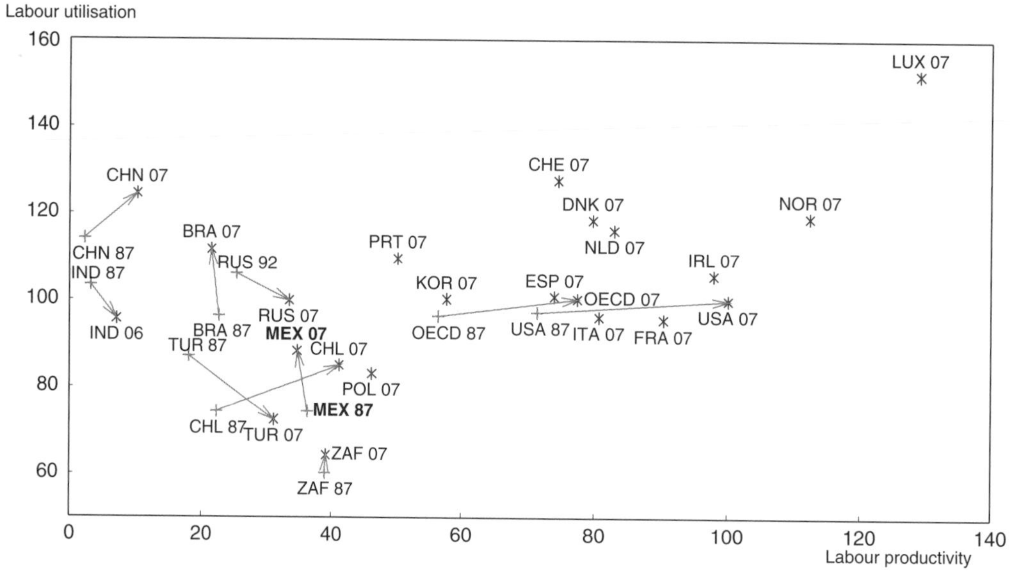

1. This figure shows the decomposition of GDP per capita into its two principal components, which are Labour Productivity (LU) and Labour Utilisation (LP). Countries in the left upper corner combine a high degree of LU with a low degree of LP. All contributions are expressed in relation to the USA's values in 1987. The chart also shows the change of positions between 1987 and 2007 for the selected countries (for Russia it shows changes between 1992 and 2007), the USA and the OECD.

Source: OECD, National Accounts; World Bank, WDI; International Monetary Fund, WEO; United Nations, UNSD.

StatLink ⟨⟨⟨ http://dx.doi.org/10.1787/684727470505

constantly increasing after the 1995 Tequila crisis, labour utilisation has actually been moving in the opposite direction from each 5-year period to the next (Table 4.3).

What do models tell about factors that hold back Mexico's growth rate?

Cross-country panel data models suggests that Mexico's slow catch up with the OECD countries was due historically to weak structural and macroeconomic policies. Mexico's growth performance is analyzed out of sample with several cross-country and panel data models (Annex 4.A3).[4] They indicate that, all else equal, in view of the income gap (transitional convergence), Mexico's growth should have been 1.3% per annum higher than in the OECD countries between 1981 and 1999. In practice it was 1.9% lower (Figure 4.8). The positive convergence effect was more than offset by weaker structural and macroeconomic stabilisation policies, which are estimated to have reduced Mexican per capita growth by 1.8% compared to the OECD group. Country specific effects, external conditions and cyclical reversion played a minor role in explaining the differences over the whole sample period. However, cyclical reversion played a stronger role in boosting Mexican growth and explaining its relatively strong performance from 1996 to 1999 following the Tequila crisis.

From 1981 to 1999, the growth difference with emerging markets was mainly due to weaker macroeconomic stabilization and transitional convergence effects. The former explain between –0.4% and –1.5% and the latter about –1.0% of the difference in growth between Mexico and other emerging markets. When compared to the high-growth emerging markets, the results show that the main difference with Chile, Korea, and Malaysia was their superior structural policy setting. The difference with the lower-income

Figure 4.8. **Annual average GDP per capita growth performance**
1981-1999

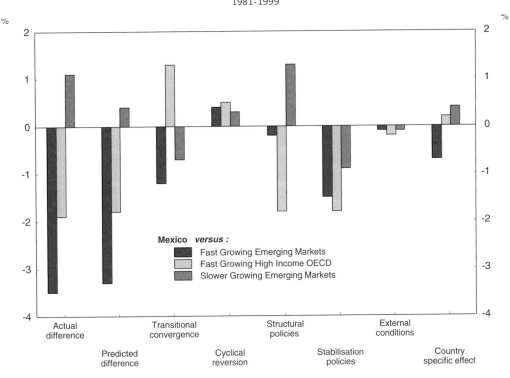

Source: OECD simulations using the Loayza, Fajnzylber and Calderón (2005) model.

StatLink ⟪▥⟫ http://dx.doi.org/10.1787/684741768107

countries in this group, such as India, was their stronger convergence effect than in Mexico. When compared with the slower growing emerging markets, Mexico appears to have had stronger structural policy settings but weaker macroeconomic stabilisation and transitional convergence effects.

The comparison highlights the importance of both structural and macroeconomic policies for economic growth performance. Mexico's progress in this in recent years is confirmed by the data (Figure 4.9). Macroeconomic stabilisation started to contribute positively to growth since the mid-1990's relative to emerging markets and also had a smaller drag on catch-up with the fast growing high income OECD countries. This is further confirmed by extending the data to 2000-07.[5]

The model suggests that more progress with structural reform remains key to faster growth. Lower inflation and the prevention of financial crises were important in raising the growth rate while slow progress with structural reform worked in the opposite direction. This suggests that if Mexico is to grow faster, it is especially in this area that improvements need to be made. Both higher-income, fast-growing OECD countries and the fast growing emerging markets have a stronger structural policy contribution to growth than Mexico. When the structural policy contribution is broken down further, Mexico's key weaknesses are in education, infrastructure and financial market development compared with both the high income OECD countries and the fast-growing emerging economies (Chile, Korea and Malaysia). Trade integration, governance and the size of government are less important (Figure 4.10) compared to the OECD group. The weakness in financial market development, as indicated by the domestic credit-to-GDP ratio, highlights an important link between

Figure 4.9. **Relative contribution of macroeconomic stabilisation policies to GDP per capita growth**

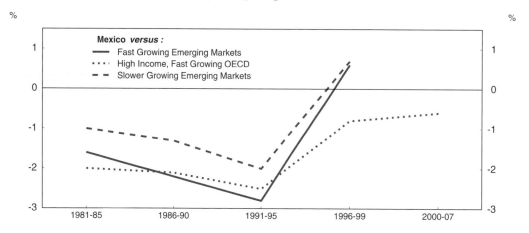

Source: OECD simulations using the Loayza, Fajnzylber and Calderón (2005) model.

StatLink 🔗 http://dx.doi.org/10.1787/684808860180

Figure 4.10. **Relative contribution of structural policies to GDP per capita growth**
1981-99

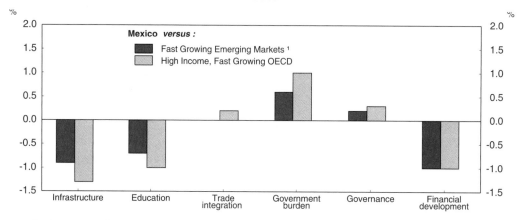

1. Malaysia, Korea and Chile.

Source: OECD simulations using the Loayza, Fajnzylber and Calderón (2005) model.

StatLink 🔗 http://dx.doi.org/10.1787/684823313605

macroeconomic stability and structural policy drivers. Mexico's previous financial crisis contributed significantly to this structural problem as banks spent a long time repairing their balance sheets.

Estimations based on a cross-country growth model by Sala-i-Martin (1997) between 1960 and 1992 show that initial conditions and, again, weak structural policies largely explain Mexico's weak growth performance. Mexico's low level of human capital, measured by the primary school enrolment rate in 1960, is the largest factor in its underperformance. In addition, four important policy-related variables – the years of openness of the economy, the rule of law, the proportion of machinery and equipment in investment and state control of the economy – were also important in explaining Mexico's weaker growth during that period. Although the model is estimated for a period that ended 15 years ago, subsequent developments can be used to determine whether the variables are still relevant and whether the government's current policies are helping to deal with the problems.

Estimates with another model by Sala-i-Martin, Doppelhoffer and Miller (2004) also point to the importance of initial conditions in terms of a large convergence gap. The model uses an averaging technique to detect which among numerous potential variables best explains growth. The exercise shows that initial conditions were important in Mexico, especially compared with the faster growing OECD with which Mexico had a large convergence gap. At the same time, this disadvantaged it versus the 10 fastest growing emerging markets, as they were generally poorer than Mexico in 1960. The weak outcome is explained by Mexico's relative poor human capital stock in 1960 vis-à-vis both groups. In addition, human capital measured by life expectancy explains weaker growth vis-à-vis the faster growing OECD countries. Only one policy related variable, openness, measured as the number of years the economy has been open between 1950 and 1994, of the 21 chosen stands out in explaining Mexico's poor performance relative to faster growing countries from 1960-1996. Simulations with the two models above identify convergence as the most important factor that should be contributing to higher growth in Mexico vis-à-vis the OECD countries. This seems obvious given the large income gap.

Studies on determinants of growth in Mexico and comparator countries also point to structural weaknesses such as lack of competition as important determinants of weak growth performance. Phillips, Mehrez and Moissinac (2006) compared Mexico with fast-growing countries and found that it has relative weaknesses in physical capital accumulation and in structural factors such as financial development, infrastructure, rule of law (including contract enforcement), education attainments and competition. The findings are in line with other more general growth studies. An extensive panel data regression analysis of growth in the OECD countries also identified the macroeconomic environment, trade openness and financial market development as particularly important for explaining growth differences (Bassanini, Scarpetta, Hemmings, 2001).

An important factor explaining slow convergence in Mexico is restrictive product market regulations (PMR) that tend to capture many structural weaknesses. Mexico's PMR level is one of the most restrictive in the OECD (Figure 4.11). PMRs reduce competition that would motivate firms to enhance productivity by adopting new technologies and processes. Regulation can also have "knock-on" effects on non-regulated sectors of the economy that use the output of the regulated sectors as intermediate inputs. For example, excessive regulation of the electricity sector will have effects on other sectors such as manufacturing where electricity is an important input. Conway, De Rosa et. al. (2006) using a sectoral model of labour productivity growth find that while regulation, measured by the regulatory impact indicators, does not directly lower growth, it impedes convergence towards the global technology frontier.[6] This is of particular concern for Mexico as it is the convergence process that should be boosting Mexican growth vis-à-vis high income OECD countries.

To quantify the "knock-on" effects of PMRs across the economy, OECD regulatory impact indicators were calculated for Mexico to compare them with those previously done for 21 other OECD countries (Conway and Nicoletti 2006).[7] The regulatory impact of PMR in Mexico is above the OECD median for all industries, except in real estate and business services. The largest negative impact is in the network industries (electricity, gas and

Figure 4.11. **Product market regulation**[1]

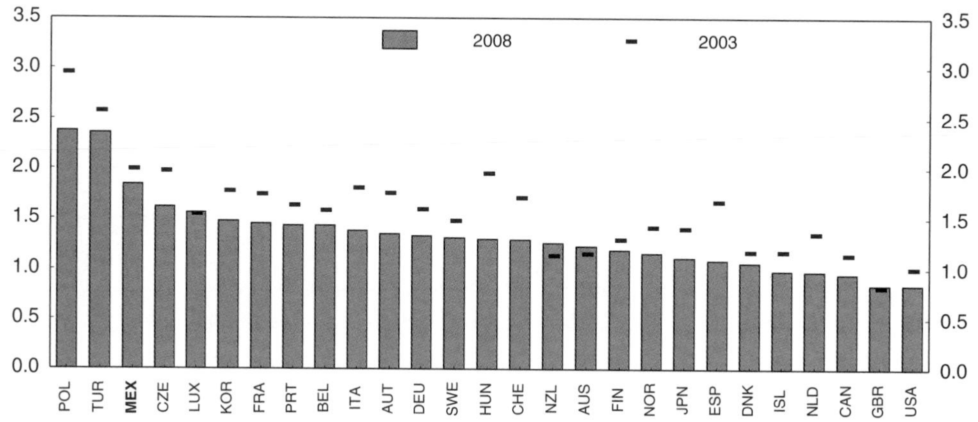

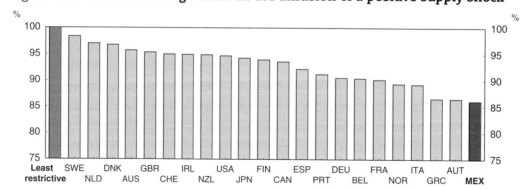

1. Overall indicator, the scale of the indicator is 0-6 from least to most restrictive of competition.
Source: OECD, Product Market Regulation database.

StatLink http://dx.doi.org/10.1787/685025475866

water) where the regulatory impact of PMR in Mexico is fourfold compared to the OECD median).

Frontier model simulations confirm that weak anti-competition regulations have a large negative impact on convergence in Mexico. A simulation by Conway and De Rosa for 21 other OECD countries is repeated to include Mexico.[8] It is carried out from a steady state in which the level of productivity is the same across all sectors and countries, to which a one-off positive shift in the world productivity frontier of equal size in all sectors is imposed. The shock results in the same productivity gap in all countries and sectors initially but the subsequent speed of convergence towards the frontier depends on the relative restrictiveness of anti-competitive regulations in each industry across countries (Figure 4.12). Mexico has the slowest convergence in the sample.

Figure 4.12. **The effect of regulation on the diffusion of a positive supply shock**[1, 2]

1. The increase in the level of aggregate labour productivity 5 years after a positive supply shock to the world technological frontier of an equal magnitude in each sector. The data are expressed as a percentage of the response that would occur in a country with regulation that is the least restrictive.
2. Productivity is derived as the value-added weighted average of industry-level productivities.
Source: OECD calculations using model estimates from Conway, De Rosa et al.(2006).

StatLink http://dx.doi.org/10.1787/685027478214

Another simulation comparing the United States and Mexico also shows that Mexican productivity would be higher with a lower level of PMR. The model compares the actual industry labour productivity gaps between the United States and Mexico in 2005 assuming that US labour productivity remained constant at 2005 levels. It is simulated under two scenarios – Mexico retains the level of PMRs prevailing in 2003, and it moves to the least restrictive PMR existing in the OECD across all industries in 2005. This shows that after 10 years Mexico's labour productivity level would be about 12% higher if it introduced regulatory reforms. Even after 20 years of catch-up it would still have a labour productivity level 8% higher than if it retained 2003 PMR levels (Figure 4.13).

Figure 4.13. **Simulated convergence of labour productivity towards the United States**

Convergence with least restrictive PMR – convergence with Mexico's PMR in 2003

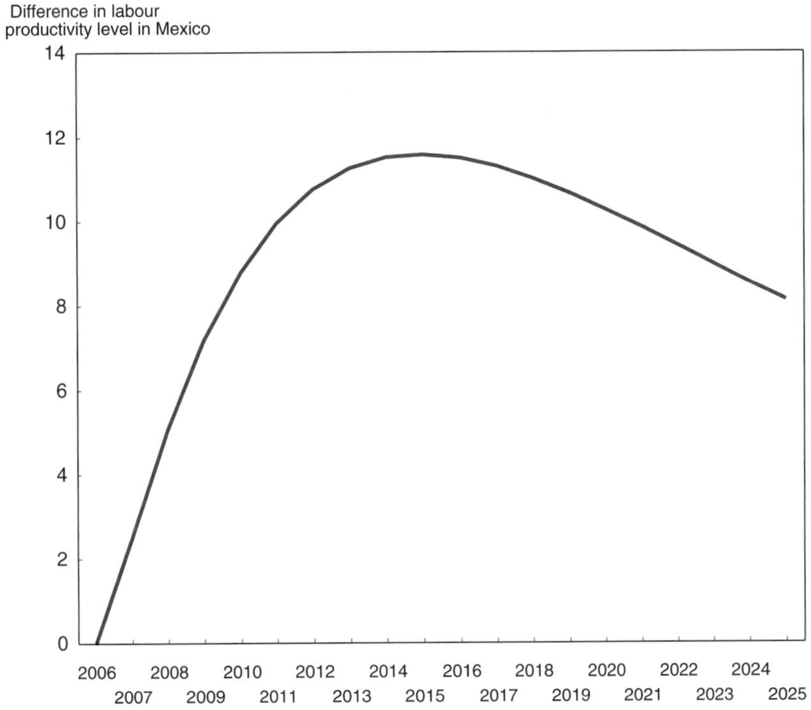

Difference in labour productivity level in Mexico

Source: OECD calculations using model estimates from Conway, De Rosa et al. (2006).

StatLink 🔗 http://dx.doi.org/10.1787/685046636823

Where to from here? Policy priorities for lifting growth further

To boost Mexico's weak but improving growth performance the above analysis points to both macroeconomic and structural factors. Mexico has improved its macroeconomic stability in recent years, which partly explains the improvements in its growth performance this decade (see Chapter 1). However, structural reform to boost productivity seems to have been slower and the list of needed reforms is long. The recent significant reductions in import tariffs should help the economy take fuller advantage of trade and investment integration, which could be a relative strength for Mexico given its geographic location. Reforms introduced in the past two years, including those to promote competition and transparency in the financial sector and, to a lesser extent in telecommunications, will also stimulate the dynamism of the economy. Despite this progress, further reforms are needed to boost overall and within-sector productivity. Relative weaknesses in education (see Chapter 3), infrastructure, financial development, the rule of law, as well as a lack of competition arising from overly restrictive product market regulation and excessive state control come out in various studies as explaining why Mexico has not grown as fast as other countries. Science, technology and innovation policies can also be important over time as noted in the OECD *Review of Innovation Policy* in Mexico.[9]

Going forward it is important to identify most relevant growth-boosting reforms while taking into account ongoing efforts. Some of the model estimations reflect time periods when many reforms were not yet in place in Mexico and may thus give a distorted picture of today's priorities. Circumstances and policies change and problems that held growth back in the past are not always relevant for the performance of the economy going forward. Furthermore, the areas identified in the above simulations as restricting growth in Mexico are not exhaustive but rather pointing to some clear relative weakness compared to faster-growing countries. There are a number of other policies and factors that are likely to influence growth and will need to be addressed if Mexico is to grow faster. These include, for example, security, inequality (Box 4.2), restrictive employment regulations and

---

Box 4.2. **Growth and Inequality – Lessons for Mexico from the current literature**

Figure 4.14. **Inequality in Mexico : Across countries and over time**

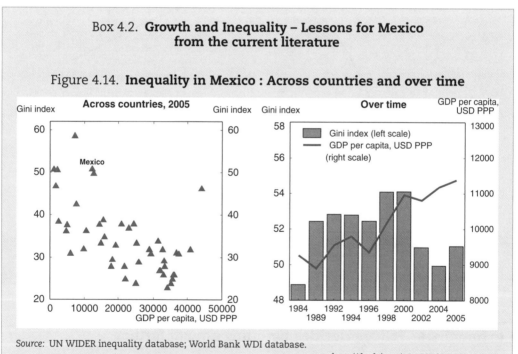

Source: UN WIDER inequality database; World Bank WDI database.

StatLink ⬛📄 http://dx.doi.org/10.1787/685058425468

Views have evolved over time on the links between growth and inequality but there seems to be no clear causality from one to the other. Kuznets hypothesized in the 1950's that in the initial phases of development income inequality increases, as an economy moves from an agricultural to an industrial economy. As the economy matures and the industrial sector expands, income inequality decreases. More recent theories suggest that growth driven by skill biased technical change may increase income inequality as wages of lower skilled workers decline in relative terms. However, the consensus view is that there is no robust causal link from growth to inequality (Easterly, 1999, Dollar & Kraay, 2002).

Box 4.2. **Growth and Inequality – Lessons for Mexico
from the current literature** *(cont.)*

Another strand of literature has focused on the inequality-to-growth link, but with no conclusive evidence. Inequality would promote growth through the accumulation of physical capital as rich individuals have higher savings rates, and capital indivisibilities require large-scale private investments and tend to improve incentive structures. On the other hand, inequality is harmful for growth if it reduces accumulation of human capital in the presence of credit constraints, and increases demand for redistribution through taxation and sociopolitical unrest. However, empirical evidence on these links is inconclusive. Some find that initial inequality has a negative effect on subsequent growth (Alesina and Rodrik, 1994, Perotti, 1996) in pooled cross-country regressions, but the effect becomes insignificant or positive when unobserved cross-country heterogeneity is taken into account (Barro, 2000 and Forbes, 2000)

Two of the channels highlighted by the literature on the relationship between inequality and growth are of particular relevance for Mexico. The literature on the missing growth-to-inequality link implies that growth in per capita income alone may not be sufficient to reduce inequality in Mexico. While cross-country evidence suggests that reducing income inequality would not be sufficient to boost long-term growth in Mexico, inequality can affect growth in Mexico by reducing human capital accumulation through poor education outcomes (Galor and Zeira (1993), and by increasing sociopolitical instability (Alesina and Perotti, 1996).

Figure 4.15. **Inequality and political stability**

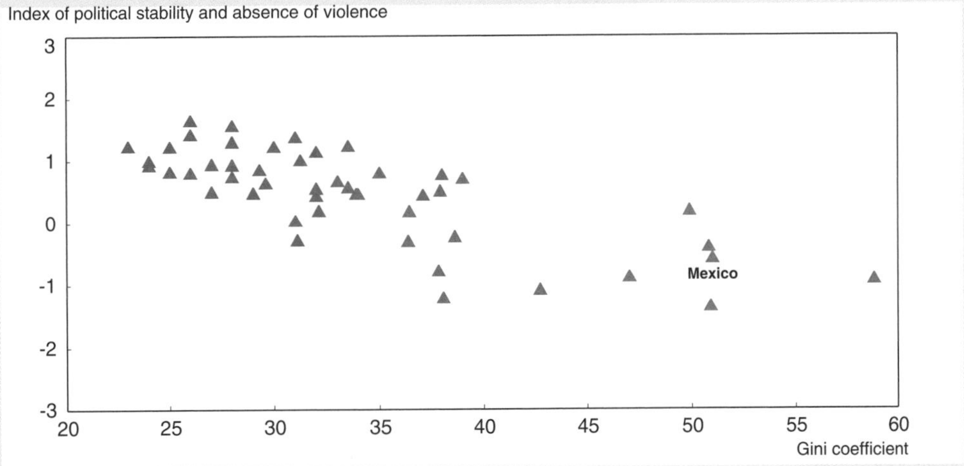

Source: UN WIDER inequality database; World Bank governance indicators.

StatLink ᴍᴤᴾ http://dx.doi.org/10.1787/685062558650

Therefore, growth in Mexico could benefit from specific measures aimed at reducing inequality. While reducing inequality through direct income transfers may not be possible due to a weak tax base, the government can take other targeted measures. Improving access to secondary education to poor families can ensure that inequality does not prevent low-income individuals from accumulating human capital. This can be done by expanding the *Oportunidades* programme of cash grants to parents in exchange for school attendance, and facilitating the transition from school to the labour market. These efforts would also help reduce sociopolitical instability and violence in the long run.

innovation policies.[10] This section examines developments, both during and subsequent to the model estimation periods, to identify which variables remain relevant for lifting incomes in Mexico. It also identifies current government policies that have improved Mexico's growth and where policy action still needs to be taken.

Structural reforms that can be implemented quickly can also have short-term pay-offs in helping countries exit from the financial crisis in addition to longer-term growth benefits. Reforms that help sustain demand or improve productivity and competitiveness to help take advantage of the recovery are particularly important and can bring double dividends. The former include expenditures on labour-market policies, for example to increase training, education and reducing entry barriers to business (see Chapter 1). These can boost demand by transferring income to poorer households or improve employment prospects and growth by enhancing future productivity (OECD 2009a).

Macroeconomic stability

Broadly sound macroeconomic policies are contributing to good growth performance and should continue. Macroeconomic management of the economy has improved substantially since the 1995 Tequila crisis, as evidenced by a drop in inflation, small current account and fiscal deficits, low public and foreign debt, and a comfortable reserve cover (Chapter 1). Mexico's commitment to macroeconomic stability, including an independent inflation targeting central bank and fiscal prudence are important cornerstones of this improved performance and should continue.

Openness and trade and investment integration

Lack of trade integration has ceased to be a major hindrance to growth. Trade integration was an issue for growth prior to the early 1990s, but subsequent liberalization episodes (WTO 1986, NAFTA 1994, unilateral actions) have substantially increased the share of trade in GDP – from 39% in 1990 to 67% in 2008. Simulations with the Loayza *et al.* model show that lack of trade integration is no longer a relative weakness *vis-à-vis* comparators. Furthermore, openness helped Mexico stage a rapid recovery after the 1995 crisis by facilitating strong export growth (Cerra and Saxena, 2005, Tornell, Westermann and Martinez, 2004).[11]

Continuing with recent progress on more liberalization could make trade and investment integration more of a strength for growth and facilitate a rapid recovery from the crisis. The strong export growth in the late 1990s has weakened more recently. Similarly, FDI that has been close to the OECD average in terms of GDP is on a declining trend and below rates seen in other catching-up countries in the OECD. It is also concentrated in the manufacturing and finance sectors where barriers to investment are lower. At end 2008, Mexico's trade policy was more restrictive (on a combined measure of tariff and non-tariff barriers) than the OECD average and other emerging market countries (Haugh, Rocha and Jamin, 2008). The substantial reductions in tariffs announced in December 2008 are a step in the right direction. Investment barriers, including those for FDI, remain higher than in most OECD and Latin American countries (OECD, 2009). Further opening up of sector to private investment and to FDI would contribute to increase productivity. This would be the case particularly in service and infrastructure sectors, including energy, transport and telecommunications that provide inputs for the whole economy. Further reforms to boost trade and investment integration could reinforce openness as a relative strength for growth in Mexico, improve its ability to take advantage of recovery when it comes, and even help offset other disadvantages that are more difficult to remedy.

Given its assets, including geographical position, Mexico's potential gains from further trade and investment liberalisation are high. Equations estimated across a panel of OECD countries indicate that an increase in trade integration of 10 percentage points of GDP (combined measure of export intensity and import penetration) would raise output per working-age person by 4% (OECD, 2003). OECD estimates also suggest that reducing FDI restrictions to those prevailing in the least restrictive country in the OECD would increase the stock of FDI in Mexico by 50% (Nicoletti *et al.*, 2003), with consequent benefits for growth through technological transfer, increased competition and innovation.

Financial market development

Boosting Mexico's low financial development should also help growth. Despite progress, Mexico's financial sector remains underdeveloped compared to emerging market peers. Domestic credit to the private sector at about 20% of GDP is low compared to countries with similar income levels. For example, Chile and China (Figure 4.16b) were close to 80%. Adding credit directly from abroad increases the ratio only to 25% of GDP. Similarly, while stock market capitalisation has grown from 32% of GDP in 1996 to 42% in 2006, it still remains well below the OECD average of 121% and levels in other fast growing emerging markets such as Chile, China, India and Korea (Figure 4.16c).

Building on recent reforms Mexico can further promote financial development (IMF, 2007). Mexico introduced reforms to improve the regulation of the financial sector early in the decade and credit growth accelerated until the recent turmoil especially to households. Given the large gap between financial sector depth in Mexico and faster-growing countries, Mexico should reinforce reforms in this area, including those related to the rule of law (see below). At the same time, it is important that any expansion in financial sector depth is sustainable and that the government maintains fiscal discipline as public-sector debt has crowded out lending to the private sector in the past.

The rule of law and enforcing credit contracts

The rule of law remains the greatest outstanding growth-related problem in Mexico according to the Sala-i-Martin 1997 model. A comparison of Mexico with the average rule of law prevailing with the 10 fastest growing countries in the model shows that Mexico's rule of law has worsened between 1996 and 2007 in absolute and relative terms. The enforceability of contracts, a part of the rule of law that is important for the business environment and the financial sector in particular, is weak. This is evidenced, for example, by much higher debt recovery costs than the OECD average and many other emerging markets, including Argentina, Brazil, Chile and China in 2007 (Figure 4.17). This may also have contributed to the low level of financial development. Recent government estimates also show that security problems are reducing annual growth by about 1 percentage point. Increasing security in Colombia, for example, has been shown to have substantial growth effects.

Education and human capital

Improving human capital by further reforms in the education system remains another priority for growth with positive spillovers to sustaining demand during the crisis (Chapter 3). The model simulations showed that relative weakness in human capital

Figure 4.16. **Domestic credit to the private sector and stock market capitalisation**

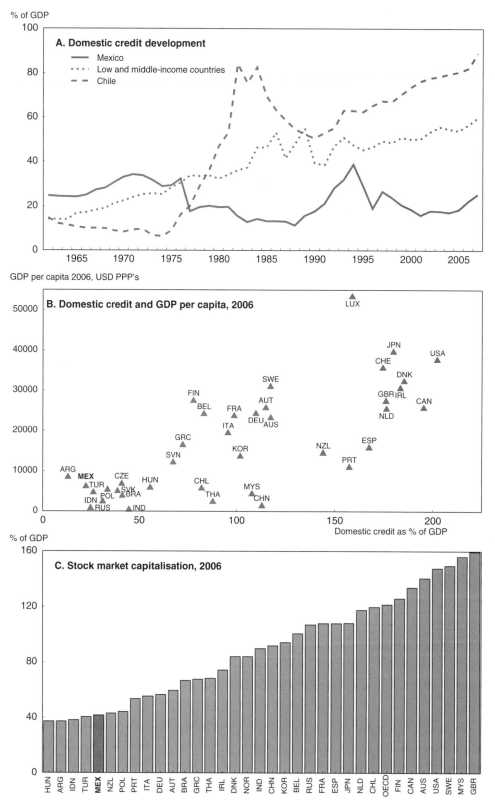

Source: World Bank, World Development Indicators.

StatLink ⟲ http://dx.doi.org/10.1787/685073052031

Figure 4.17. **Cost of enforcing contracts, 2007**

As per cent of total debt values

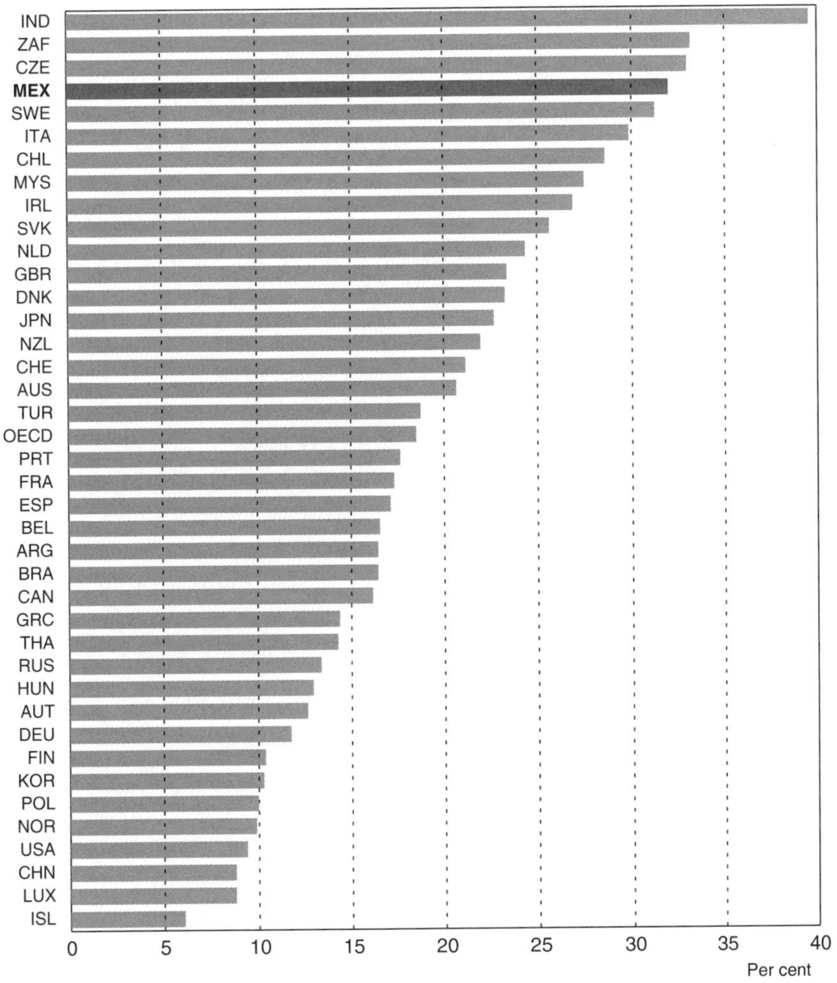

Source: World Bank, World Bank Cost of Doing Business, 2008.

StatLink ᵃᵍ⁵ᵖ http://dx.doi.org/10.1787/685084181026

explains much of the slower growth performance compared to fast-growing countries. Indeed, human capital in the working age population (as measured by average years of schooling) is the lowest in the OECD and other emerging markets despite Mexico spending more than the OECD average on education as a share of GDP. Furthermore, the education system has not generated the large inter-generational increases in educational attainments observed in faster-growing economies such as Greece or Korea (Guichard, 2005, OECD, 2007). Extending education coverage would also help sustain demand and reduce unemployment among the young during the crisis. Only about two-thirds of the relevant age group attend secondary school.

Recent reforms to improve educational quality should be complemented by improving access to education further. Mexico has initiated innovative reforms in education through the *Oportunidades programme* that aimed at targeted interventions to improve access to schooling of lower income groups. This may have contributed to the increase in secondary enrolment rates between 1996 and 2005 after stagnation between 1981 and 1995. This growth is similar to other fast-growing emerging markets. However, in terms of educational quality, Mexico is lagging both OECD and emerging market countries (as measured by PISA scores). Faster-growing emerging markets such as Chile, China, Poland and Turkey are generating better education outcomes relative to their income level than Brazil and Mexico (Figure 3.1). Raising educational attainment and particularly the quality of educational outcomes in Mexico should remain a policy priority if Mexico is to lift its growth rate further.

Regulation and competition

Convergence and recovery would also be boosted by increasing competition by reducing product market regulations. Apart from directly restricting competition, the regulatory framework is not facilitating new entrants. For example, it is not providing adequate, non-discriminatory third party access to networks in areas such as telecommunications and railways (OECD, 2007). The result is an economy with high levels of concentration and ineffective competition in many sectors. Coupled with restrictive foreign trade and investment policies this is reducing both the ability and incentive to innovate and adopt new technology and practices from abroad which are important for higher productivity growth and rapid recovery. This applies in particular to telecommunications. Deregulation was among the most important determinants of the growth advantage of the United States and other English-speaking and small EU countries over the past two decades (Nicoletti and Scarpetta, 2005). However, this may not be sufficient to generate competition, especially in network industries such as telecommunications, which underlines the importance of a regulatory regime that facilitates entry and new acquisitions.

Mexico's decision to conduct a project to strengthen competitiveness is an important step to achieve higher levels of investment, employment and growth. This process involves identifying and modifying regulations and policies that unnecessarily restrict competition, and evaluates the regulatory and legal difficulties facing enterprises, using the OECD Competition Assessment Toolkit (Box 4.3). The large number and complexity of laws and regulations that impede competition mean that an ongoing commitment will be required to gain the maximum return from this strategy.[12] The experience in Australia, where a similar process was conducted, suggests that such an effort is well justified by the subsequent growth benefits, which are likely to be substantial. Indeed, Australia outperformed the OECD for several years in both GDP and GDP per capita growth terms since the commencement of the regulatory review there in 1993. Its performance is currently less impressive and the government attributes that at least in part to a reduced emphasis on pro-competitive reforms lately. Consequently, Australia plans to ratchet up its pro-competition actions in the years to come.

Reforms to boost access to network industries can help sustain the competitive advantage gained from the recent real depreciation and help a rapid recovery when world trade picks up. The productivity gains can be substantial according to the studies reviewed. The government has taken important recent steps to improve competition especially in the telecommunications area by introducing number portability and lowering interconnection charges. In addition, plans to carry out additional auctions of radiospectrum frequencies and of new fiber optic networks should further promote competition in the sector. Additional reforms would complement those envisaged by the Ministry of Economy to

> ### Box 4.3. **Reducing unnecessary restraints on competition using the competition assessment toolkit**
>
> The Mexican government represented by the Ministry of the Economy signed in July 2007 a memorandum of understanding with the OECD to increase Mexico's competitiveness based on two pillars: strengthening competition and improving the regulatory framework. Both pillars developed technical and highly experienced task forces to carry out their process. The competition pillar is coordinated by the Federal Competition Commission (COFECO) and the other group by the Ministry of the Economy. The competition process is conducted using OECD's Competition Assesment Toolkit (OECD, 2007b). The toolkit contains a checklist that signals when there is a potential competition problem that should be investigated in-more depth (along the lines of those regularly conducted by Competition Authorities). The checklist identifies potential problems if the policy, law or regulation will:
>
> - limit the number or range of suppliers, *e.g.* establishes a license process as an operation requirement; and/or;
>
> - limit the ability of suppliers to compete, *e.g.* significantly raises production costs of new entrants relative to incumbents; and/or;
>
> - reduce the incentive of suppliers to compete vigorously; reduce mobility of consumers between suppliers.
>
> If a more in-depth investigation reveals that there is an undue restriction on competition, the toolkit contains advice on alternatives that may offset or mitigate potential harm to competition while still achieving the policy objective of the original law/regulation.
>
> Additionally, the project uses the Standard Cost Model to cost administrative burdens, to inform and generate measures of regulatory improvement and administrative simplification.
>
> The review process is being conducted by a group of both economic and legal experts, who provide advice on where problems lie and possibilities for resolving them. The Ministry of the Economy then makes recommendations for regulatory reform to a competitiveness cabinet of ministers. Ensuring the success of this process in eliminating unnecessary restraints on competition and lifting productivity growth will require both ongoing resourcing and ensuring that there is a durable mechanism for implementation.

create a one-stop-shop for business registrations and aid to start-up companies. By attracting investment to new activities the reform would also help the recovery.

Infrastructure

Increasing infrastructure levels can have positive effects on economic growth and sustaining activity in the downturn. Progress has also been made, with an important increase in infrastructure investment from an average of 3% of GDP in 2000-2006 to 5% for 2009, but it will take time to close the infrastructure gap, as provision in Mexico is low by OECD standards (OECD, 2008) and Mexico faces a number of challenges in this area. In telecommunications, Mexico tends to underperform other emerging market peers with fewer mainline telephones, fixed, mobile and broadband subscriptions per capita and lower international internet bandwidth per capita (Figure 4.18). Road and rail provision remains relatively limited, even compared with other emerging markets, as evidenced by

Figure 4.18. **Fixed and mobile subscribers**
Per 100 people, 2005

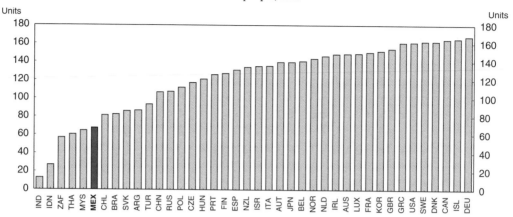

Source: World Bank, World Development Indicators.

StatLink ᘎᗏ http://dx.doi.org/10.1787/685104570720

the relatively low density of the networks as measured by lines per square kilometre (Figure 4.19a and b). Despite having lower population densities Argentina, Brazil and Chile have higher road and rail network densities than Mexico. At the same time, existing investments in Mexico seem unbalanced, as many areas are without roads and much is concentrated close to the US border with high user fees. Road congestion, as indicated by the number of vehicles per road kilometre, is also relatively high. In energy, while total electricity generation capacity appears to be adequate or even on the high side in per capita terms at Mexico's income levels,[13] the reserve margin (total capacity in excess of peak load demand) is high by OECD standards.[14] Prices also remain relatively high compared with other OECD countries in electricity and telecommunications (OECD, 2007) suggesting that benefits from greater competition such as more innovation and higher productivity are lacking in these sectors. This means that apart from increasing public investment, promoting competition can also help improve both the quantity and quality of infrastructure in Mexico as pointed out by the PMR results discussed earlier.

Concluding remarks

Mexico has made some progress in boosting growth but not enough for satisfactory catch-up. Mexico's reforms, especially those to increase macroeconomic-stability and open the economy to greater trade and investment over the last decade have paid off. They have facilitated strong export-led growth following the 1995 financial crisis and reduced macroeconomic imbalances and vulnerabilities with some positive impact on growth. Mexico now enjoys a level of macroeconomic stability that rivals many higher income countries in the OECD. The economy has become far more integrated in the world economy than two decades ago, increasing the pressure on firms to innovate and exploit the possibilities for technology transfer, especially in the more open manufacturing sector. Taken together, these factors have helped increase GDP per capita growth from near zero in the late 1980s to around 2% in the 2002-07 period. Although this is around the OECD average, it is too low to allow rapid convergence to living standards in the higher-income OECD countries. As an emerging market with a large income gap to the rest of the OECD,

Figure 4.19. **Network density, 2005**[1]

Kilometres per 1000 square kilometres

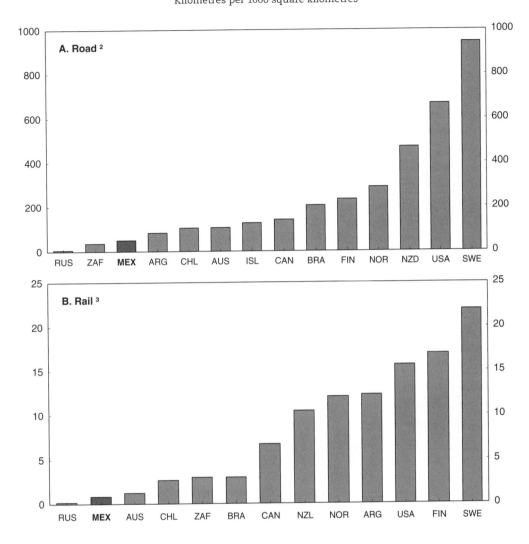

1. Countries with a population density below Mexico's.
2. 2000 for Chile and Russia.
3. 1990 for Argentina and 1998 for New Zealand.

Source: World Bank, World Development Indicators database; North American Transport Statistics.

StatLink ᓂᔅᒲ *http://dx.doi.org/10.1787/685116350148*

and a long border with the world's largest single market, Mexico should be doing much better than the average.

However, convergence to higher living standards is far from automatic and requires addressing structural weaknesses more rigorously. A comparison of Mexico's performance with better performing emerging markets and OECD countries reveals that Mexico's weaker growth is largely driven by lower labour productivity growth. To raise labour productivity, more reforms are needed on the structural front. Relative weaknesses in competition, education, the rule of law, infrastructure, and financial development are areas that explain Mexico's poorer performance relative to faster growing countries in the past. There have been important improvements in several of these areas, but efforts along these lines need to continue going forward (see Annex 4.A1, and OECD 2009). Further opening up the economy to higher private investment, both domestic and foreign, would also contribute to higher productivity.

Although reforms are needed on a broad front, rapid progress with limited resources can be obtained by focusing reforms on increasing competition. Mexico also needs to monitor and ensure previous reforms in areas such as financial markets deliver their aims. It should also complement this with further policy change to deal with persisting structural weakness. Recent OECD work contains detailed recommendations for improving education outcomes, lifting competition and improving infrastructure, increasing the benefits from international trade and investment, especially in the telecommunication sector.

Box 4.4. Policy recommendations for boosting growth and spurring economic recovery

Boost competition to enhance productivity, growth and recovery

- Increase competition in the main network industries–electricity, gas, water, telecommunications and transport – through regulatory action.

- Further liberalise investment regimes by reducing both barriers to domestic and foreign investment. Enhance trade links with Asia to diversify trade.

- Increasing competition and reducing entry barriers in telecommunications further is of particular importance for the diffusion of new technologies.

Sustain demand and improve competitiveness with a better infrastructure

- Focus on sectors with rapid pay-offs such as education (coverage and quality, see Chapter 3), and transport networks (road, rail and ports).

- Continue to increase infrastructure spending provided capacity constraints allow it.

Notes

1. Mexico's growth record should be compared to both OECD and emerging economies to get an appropriate benchmark in line with income levels. As a member of the OECD, Mexico's performance is regularly compared with the mostly higher-income members of the OECD. See, for example, Scarpetta, Bassanini, Pilat and Schreyer (2000). This section extends this analysis by comparing Mexico with a peer group of large emerging market economies (defined here as those "emerging" in the world economy through greater participation in world trade and investment flows) such as Brazil, Chile, China, India, Russia, South Africa, and Turkey. They can be better comparators than OECD countries as their level of GDP per capita and development issues faced are more similar to Mexico's. They are also, like Mexico, pursuing economic reforms designed to assist convergence with the higher-income OECD countries.

2. Total and sectoral labour productivity in Mexico is compared with 3 groups of countries, slower growing emerging markets (Brazil and Venezuela), fast growing emerging markets (Chile, India, Korea, Malaysia, Thailand) and fast growing, high-income OECD countries (Australia, Finland, Ireland, United Kingdom, United States).

3. Data for emerging countries was sourced from the ten sector database available at the Groningen Growth and Development Centre and is downloadable at *www.ggdc.net/dseries/10-sector.html*. See Timmer and De Vires (2007). Data for the OECD countries was sourced from the EU Klems database, March 2008 release, and is downloadable from *www.euklems.net/*. See Timmer, O'Mahony & van Ark (2007).

4. These were chosen based on whether they included Mexico and emerging markets, policy variables and had accessible data. The Loayza, Fajnzylber and Calderón (2005) cross-country panel

data model was used to compare Mexico with three groups with differing growth records—fast growing high income OECD (the United States, United Kingdom, Australia, Finland, Ireland and Spain), fast growing emerging markets (China, India, Malaysia, Thailand, Korea, Turkey, Chile and Egypt), and slower growing emerging markets (Ecuador, Paraguay, Venezuela, South Africa, Argentina and Brazil).

5. 5. The model estimates could not be extended beyond 1999 to other specifications as relevant data is not available for the emerging market group.

6. In the model, labour productivity growth is a function of improvements in the global productivity frontier, the gap to the frontier and the speed of convergence, and in some versions, measures of human and physical capital. The model was estimated for 21 OECD countries across 39 industries.

7. The indicator measures the regulatory impact on 11 industries in Mexico as the weighted average of anti-competitive PMR in 6 non-manufacturing sectors—electricity, gas and water, post and telecommunications, transport and storage, wholesale and retail trade, other business activities. The weights are proportional to the intermediate input requirements of each of the 11 industries from each of the non-manufacturing sectors. For example, an industry such as paper manufacturing which uses a relatively high amount of electricity as an intermediate input will have a higher weight on PMR in the electricity sector than another industry where less electricity is required per unit of final output. In comparison with the rest of the OECD, the regulatory impact of PMR in the non-manufacturing sectors is relatively high both in the sector and in those such as manufacturing that use their services. More specifically, the weights are the input-output coefficients calculated using the 2003 input-output table (matriz insumo-producto) for Mexico available *www.inegi.gob.mx*. The PMR indicators for the non-manufacturing sectors are obtained from the OECD PMR database available at *www.oecd.org*. In some cases they are simple averages of the indicators for several sub-sectors, for example the transport indicator is the average of the PMR indicators for the airline, road and rail sectors. Figure 5 in Conway and Nicoletti (2006) contains further details. The finance PMR indicator was calculated by de Serres *et. al.* (2006) and assesses the degree to which regulation encourages or inhibits competition in banking and financial services. For the OECD countries other than Mexico the regulatory impact indicator for total manufacturing is derived by calculating an industry value-added weighted average of the regulatory impact indicator in individual manufacturing industries.

8. Coefficients from the sectoral model in Column 2, Table 1B are used in the simulations. Results for countries other than Mexico vary somewhat from the original simulations due to subsequent revisions to the regulatory impact indicators.

9. Machinery and equipment investment levels no longer appear to be lower than in faster growing countries. Mexico's proportion of machinery investment as a share of GDP between 1993 and 2007 is considerably higher than the value for the 1960-1992 period and more in line with the faster growing countries.

10. Innovation policy in Mexico is discussed in OECD (2009b).

11. A full recovery is a return to the projected trend level of GDP existing prior to the crisis.

12. In Australia's case, the National Competition Policy review examined around 1 800 laws and regulations over the 1995-2005 period.

13. Generation capacity per capita tends to be higher for richer countries as more economic activity generally requires more electricity use to some degree.

14. See OECD (2008).

Bibliography

Adrogué, R. M. Cerisola and G. Gelos (2006), "Brazil's Long-Term Growth Performance- Trying to Explain the Puzzle", IMF Working Paper, No. 06/282.

Alesina, A. and D. Rodrik, (1994), "Distributive Politics and Economic Growth", The Quarterly Journal of Economics . 109, No. 2 (May, 1994).

Barro, R. J. (2000), "Inequality and Growth in a Panel of Countries", Journal of Economic Growth, March 2000.

Bassanini, A., S. Scarpetta and P. Hemmings (2001), "Economic Growth: The Role of Policies and Institutions. Panel Data Evidence from OECD countries", OECD Economics Department Working Paper, No. 283.

Cerra, V. and S.C. Saxena (2005), "Growth Dynamics: The Myth of Economic Recovery", IMF Working Paper, No. 05/147.

Conway, P., D. De Rosa, F. Steiner and G. Nicoletti (2006), "Regulation, Competition, and Productivity Convergence", OECD Economics Department Working Paper, No. 509.

Conway, P. and G. Nicoletti (2006), "Product Market Regulation in the Non-Manufacturing Sectors of OECD Countries: Measurement and Highlights", OECD Economics Department Working Papers, No. 530.

De Serres, A., S. Kobayakawa, T. Sløk and L. Vartia (2006), "Regulation of financial systems and economic growth", OECD Economics Department Working Papers, No. 506.

Dollar, D. and A. Kraay, (2002), "Growth is good for the Poor", Journal of Economic Growth, Vol. 7.

Easterly, W. (1999), "Life during Growth", Journal of Economic Growth, Vol. 4, No. 3.

Forbes, K. J. (2000), "A reassessment of the Relationship between Inequality and Growth", The American Economic Review, Vol. 90, No. 4.

Galor, O. and J Zeira, (1993), "Income Distribution and Macroeconomics", The Review of Economic Studies, Vol. 60, No. 1.

Guichard, S. (2005), "The Education Challenge in Mexico: Delivering Good Quality Education to All", OECD Economics Department Working Papers, No. 477.

Haugh, D., B. Rocha and R. Jamin (2008), "Maximising Mexico's gains from integration in the world economy", OECD Economics Department Working Papers, No. 657.

IMF (2007), "Mexico: Financial Sector Assessment Program Update – Technical Note – Financing of the Private Sector", IMF Country Report No. 07/170.

Lenain, P. and L. Rawdanowicz (2004), "Enhancing Income Convergence in Central Europe after EU Accession," OECD Economics Department Working Papers 392.

Loayza, N., P. Fajnzylber and C. Calderón (2005), Economic Growth in Latin America and the Caribbean: Stylized Facts, Explanations and Forecasts, World Bank, Washington D.C.

Lucas, R. (1988), "On the Mechanics of Economic Development", Journal of Monetary Economics.

Phillips, S., G. Mehrez and V. Moissinac (2006), "A Survey of Conditions for Growth in Mexico:, in International Perspective", in IMF Country Report No. 06/351.

Maddison, A. (2003), "The World Economy: Historical Statistics", OECD Development Centre Studies.

Nicoletti, G.S., S. Golub, D. Hajkova, D. Mirza and K.Y. Yoo (2003), "Policies and International Integration: Influences on Trade and Foreign Direct Investment", OECD Economics Department Working Papers, No. 359.

Nicoletti, G.S., and S. Scarpetta, (2005), "Regulation and Economic Performance: Product Market Reforms and Productivity in the OECD", OECD Economics Department Working Papers, No. 460.

OECD (2003), The Sources of Economic Growth, Paris, OECD.

OECD (2007) OECD Economic Survey of Mexico, Paris, OECD.

OECD (2007a) Pisa 2006: Science Competencies for Tomorrow's World, Vol. 1, Paris, OECD.

OECD (2007b) OECD Competition Assessment Toolkit, Version 1.0, Paris, OECD.

OECD (2008) "Infrastructure Investment: Links to Growth and the Role of Public Policies", OECD Economics Department Working Paper, forthcoming.

OECD (2009a) Going for Growth, Paris, OECD.

OECD (2009b) Review of Mexico's Innovation Policies, Paris (forthcoming)

Perotti, R. (1996), "Redistribution and Non-consumption Smoothing in an Open Economy", The Review of Economic Studies, Vol. 63, No. 3.

Romer, P. (1990), "Endogenous technological change", Journal of Political Economy.

Sala-i-Martin, X. (1997), "I Just Ran Two Million Regressions", The American Economic Review, Vol. 87, No. 2, pp. 178-183.

Sala-i-Martin, X., G. Doppelhoffer and R. Miller (2004), Determinants of Long-Term Growth: A Bayesian Averaging of Classical Estimates (BACE) Approach. The American Economic Review, Vol. 94. No. 4, pp 813-835.

Scarpetta, S., A. Bassanini, D. Pilat and P. Schreyer (2000), "Economic growth in the OECD area: Recent trends at the aggregate and sectoral level", OECD Economics Department Working Paper, No. 248.

Solow, R. (1956),"6HA Contribution to the Theory of Economic Growth, The Quarterly Journal of Economics, 70, pp 65-94.

Solow, R. (1957), 7HTechnical Change and the Aggregate Production Function, The Review of Economics and Statistics, Vol. 39, pp 312-320.

Solow, R. (1961), "Note on Uzawa's two sector model of economic growth", Review of Economic Studies.

Swan, T. (1956), "Economic Growth and Capital Accumulation", Economic Record, Vol. 32, pp 334-361.

Timmer, M.P. and G. J. de Vries (2007), "A Cross-Country Database For Sectoral Employment And Productivity In Asia And Latin America, 1950-2005", Groningen Growth and Development Centre Research Memorandum GD-98.

Timmer, M.P., M. O'Mahony and B. van Ark, "The EU KLEMS Growth and Productivity Accounts: An Overview", University of Groningen and University of Birmingham available at 8Hwww.euklems.net/.

Tornell, A., F.Westermann and L.Matinez (2004), "Mexico and NAFTA's less than stellar performance", NBER Working Paper, No. 10289.

Uzawa, Hirofumi (1961), "Neutral Inventions and the Stability of Growth Equilibrium", Review of Economic Studies, February 1961, 28 (2).

ANNEX 4.A1

Progress in structural reform

This annex summarises recommendations made in previous *Surveys* and action taken since the last *Survey* was finalised in July 2007. More detailed recommendations based on analysis in this survey are listed in the relevant chapters.

Recommendations	Action taken since the previous *Survey* (July 2007)
A. Strengthening public finances	
Strengthen the fiscal framework, ensuring fiscal rules and guidelines are implemented. Save or invest extra windfall from non-renewable resources.	Upper bound on the maximum level of stabilisation funds increased for 2009.
Enhance the efficiency of public spending:.	Performance budgeting reform measures were included in the 2007 fiscal reform. Its implementation is in progress.
Increase tax revenues while reducing distortions.	The 2007 tax reform (IETU) is aimed at broadening the tax-base while improving spending efficiency. However, more reforms on non-oil taxes are needed to reduce dependency on oil revenues in the budget.
Review powers and responsibilities of sub-national governments.	The 2007 fiscal reform gave them the capacity to raise a tax on gasoline.
Limit growth of federal transfers, to give sub national government incentives to increase and execute their taxing power.	Formulas for the transfer of resources to subnational governments were modified to provide them with higher incentives to increase their own revenues.
Extend the ISSSTE pension reform to other sub-systems for public sector employees.	The pension systems of CFE and workers of IMSS were reformed in 2008.
Reform PEMEX-management, improving governance and consider allowing of joint ventures, to ensure much needed capital and technology.	PEMEX reform passed in October 2008 is being gradually implemented, mainly improving corporate governance. Performance based contracts need to be carefully designed in order to guarantee that they promote higher investment in the sector.
B. Trade and foreign investment	
Gradually reduce applied most favoured nation tariffs.	Substantial rate reduction in effect from January 1st 2009.
Reduce non-tariff barriers including: streamlining customs and technical and labelling standards; eliminating exclusive entry ports, reference prices and special registration lists for imported goods.	At the same time the rates were reduced, a wide range of measures to improve foreign trade procedures were established.
Reduce foreign ownership restrictions.	A new law reducing ownership restrictions in telecommunications was approved in the lower chamber of Congress. Approval in the Upper Chamber is pending.
Further facilitate FDI and maximise benefits from FDI.	A new law reducing ownership restrictions in telecommunications was approved in the lower chamber of Congress. Approval in the upper chamber is pending.
Strengthen the rule of law to improve business environment.	

Recommendations	Action taken since the previous *Survey* (July 2007)
C. competition, regulation and infrastructure	
Undertake broad review across the economy of legal restraints at both the federal and the state levels on competition.	The Government with the support of the OECD has launched a broad review of laws and regulations to identify and eliminate unnecessary restraints on competition. The competition commission has increased its capacity for economic analysis in competition areas.
Assign adequate resources to the Federal Competition Commission and other regulators.	No action.
Improve enforcement of competition law.	No action.
A. Energy	
Electricity: Increase competition in electricity generation, encourage private sector investment.	No action.
Gas: Continue liberalisation and opening of the sector.	Reform passed aimed at allowing competition in consumer provision.
B. Telecommunications	
Facilitate new entry and improve the regulatory framework to enhance competition.	Authorities have initiated phone number portability. Interconnection charges for mobile phone companies to fixed line companies for network traffic reduced by more than 50 percent. Permits to commercialise or resell mobile phone services granted. Additional spectrum and fibre optic network auctions have been announced.
Promote broadband including unbundling the local loop. Establish a clear legal framework for setting asset prices. Legal framework should be subject to mandatory CFC approval.	Spectrum Auction program issued in March of 2008. The Basic Technical Plan for interconnection and interoperability issued, enabling *i.e.* that end user has access to any contents, services or application provided by any operator.
C. Transport	
Border and trucking: Improve efficiency at the US border.	Pilot project with US on cross border trucking. Currently stopped by the new US administration. Authorities are working with US Government to reactivate project within the NAFTA framework.
Airlines: Proceed with privatisation of *Aeromexico* and *Mexicana* as separate entities. Increase foreign ownership ceiling in airlines to 49%.	Privatisation completed fall of 2007 and industry opened to low-cost carriers.
Roads: Encourage private sector investment.	More use of PPPs introduced. During 2009 SCT will have 38 PPPs underway.
Railways: Introduce an independent regulator and new access pricing rules to resolve interconnection disputes.	No new action.
Ports: Improve port efficiency including improving wharf to land transfer and customs procedures.	Development of logisitics activity zones (LAZ) promoted. A review of operational processes of transfer and manoeuvring of delivery-reception initiated. This has reduced the time goods spend in ports.
D. Promote a business friendly environment	
Facilitate entry and exit of firms.	Further progress in implementing the SARE (Rapid Business Start-up System). State and municipal procedures for opening a new low risk business are reduced to up to 3 days.
Reduce business costs.	One-stop-shop project initiated.
E. Enhancing human capital	
A. Increase coverage of post compulsory education	
Facilitate access of poorer students to upper secondary education.	Two new scholarship programmes initiated: "National Retention Scholarship Programme" and "Student Support Scholarship Programme".
B. Increase quality of education services	
Modernise curricula and better integrate it between levels.	No action.
Evaluate schools and publish results.	Results from the ENLACE evaluation are now published at the school level.
Review incentives for teachers.	*Alianza* reform plans to link teacher incentives to professional development and student test scores; *Carrera Magisterial* is being reformed.
C. Facilitate the transition from school to job	
Consider the introduction of apprenticeships contracts for alternation programmes.	No action.
Further strengthen vocational education.	Technical committees have been established to strengthen school-business links.

Recommendations	Action taken since the previous *Survey* (July 2007)
D. Adult training	
Continue implementation of skill certification.	Enrolment within the skill certification model has increased 45% during the 2007-2008 school year.
Strengthen public training programmes.	Work training programmes have been offered within the skill certification model during the 2007-2008 school year.
Upgrade entrepreneurial competences in small and medium-size enterprises.	Development banks (Nacional Financiera) have stepped up their programs to support SMEs, both in terms of additional financing as well as technical assistance.

F. Labour markets and poverty alleviation	
A. Labour market	
Increase the flexibility of employment regulations by easing employment protection provisions while putting in place a minimum revenue support in case of job loss.	A reform to the retirement savings system has been approved to allow workers to have greater access to the resources in their retirement accounts in case of unemployment. To make up for this, the Government's contribution was increased.
Introduce probation period, to facilitate job creation through long-term contracts.	No action.
Broaden scope for using short term contracts.	No action.
Broaden scope for using part-time contracts.	No action.
B. Review tax and benefits	
Rebalance incentives towards formal employment by reviewing the tax-benefit package to improve the reliability and efficiency of social security services. Increase attractiveness of individual pension savings (*SAR*).	Social security law reformed in favour of temporary workers in the agricultural sector, to ensure their incorporation into IMMS and earning of pension benefits.
Bring in line the public sector pension schemes with the private sector.	Public sector pensions for new employees have been aligned with the private sector.
Avoid use of payroll tax.	No new action.
C. Poverty alleviation and public security	
Adjust coverage of *Oportunidades* to include all segments of the poor population. Improve the quality of supply of health and education within program to increase effectiveness.	No action.
To aid the poor, replace subsidies by targeted cash transfers. Review effectiveness of programmes like DICONSA and LICONSA, if inefficient, refocus them or discontinue them. In general, rationalise the numerous programs with social objectives to avoid duplication and draw on synergies.	No action.
Review mix of interventions targeted at rural poverty; reinforce partnerships among actors involved in rural development.	No action.
Increase cost efficiency of IMSS health care to provide higher quality services at lower costs.	No action.
Take steps to integrate health insurance systems and split financing from providers.	No action.

ANNEX 4.A2

Data and methodology

The data used in the growth accounting and growth comparisons for emerging markets were sourced from the OECD, the International Monetary Fund (IMF), the World Bank (WB) and the United Nations (UN). Where official data were unavailable, they were supplemented by OECD country desk estimates. Databases included: the IMF's World Economic Outlook (WEO) and the World Development Indicators (WDI) from the WB and the United Nations Statistic Division (UNSD) Database from the UN.

Definition		Source	
		OECD members	Non members
GDP extension	GDP in PPP (constant 2005 $)	OECD	World Bank (WD1)
		International Monetary Fund (WEO)	
Employment		OECD	WEO
		OECD	WEO
Working age Population	Segment of the population between ages 15 and 64	Analytical Database (OECD)	United Nations (UNSD)
		OECD	UNSD
Population		OECD	UNSD
		UNSD	

Note: In some cases, there is available OECD data for non member countries. In these cases the OECD desk estimations are used instead of the alternative source used for the rest of the non member countries. Series were extended from 1980 to 2012; when the whole series was not available from the same source, they were extended extrapolating the growth rates from an alternative database.

As the goal of the work is to analyse the long-term growth of the selected countries, cyclical effects were removed by filtering all the time series using a Hodrick-Prescott Filter (HP) with lambda = 100. The HP filter becomes inaccurate at the end of a time series (Scarpetta, Bassanini, Pilat and Schreyer (2000)). To mitigate this problem, the series were extended before filtering using either OECD forecasts or extrapolation using past average growth rates.

ANNEX 4.A3

More details on the models used

The Loayza *et al.* model covers 78 countries and is estimated for 1961-1999; growth is a function of transitional convergence (the initial income gap), cyclical reversion (the size of the initial output gap), structural policies (education, financial depth, trade integration, government size, infrastructure and governance), macroeconomic stabilisation (inflation, cyclical volatility, real exchange rate overvaluation, systemic financial crises), external conditions (terms of trade shocks) and time and country dummies. The advantage of the model is the separation of the effects of structural and macroeconomic parameters from cyclical and convergence effects.

A simulation exercise was conducted to compare Mexico with 20 other economies over 1981-1999. The original model is generally good for Mexico, although it doesn't fully pick up the effects of the financial crises. The fit of the model was improved by modifying the original data for financial crises and the lag on the initial output gap for Mexico, which affects the size of macro-economic stabilisation policies. Both the original estimates and those that incorporate financial crisis effects are given to provide a range for the importance of macroeconomic stabilisation policies. An analysis of the fit of the model for Mexico revealed that, while the fit is generally good, Mexico's growth appeared to be over-estimated in the 1986-1990 and 1991-1995 periods and underestimated from 1996-2000. This appears to arise from an incorrect lag on the output gap that underestimates cyclical reversion effects in 1996-1999 and data inputs that do not fully capture the length of the 1980s debt crisis or the severity of the 1995 Tequila crisis. This is unsurprising as financial crises are mostly idiosyncratic and it is hard to generate a series that will adequately measure all crises across all countries. The lag length on the output gap and financial crises data were calibrated to better measure the effects of these events. For example, the model predicts Mexican growth between 1991-1994 well, but not for 1995 because the size of the financial crisis effect implied by the original data (the clear driver of the fall in growth in 1995) is not large enough. The financial crisis data is calibrated so that it captures the difference between growth predicted by other factors plus the average equation error for 1991-1994 and actual growth. These changes improve the fit of the model and its power of the gap between Mexican and the others in the sample, and has more intuitive signs. Changing the data inputs for financial crises affects the importance of stabilisation policies. In the extreme, stronger financial crises effects than originally incorporated in the model may explain the remainder of the gap between the model's and actual growth for Mexico in these periods and the effect of stabilisation policies will increase in parallel.

The original model data was extended to the 2000-07 period for the macroeconomic stabilisation variables (CPI, the standard deviation of the output gap, real effective exchange rate overvaluation and the frequency of systemic banking crises for Mexico and the high-income, fast growing OECD countries (United States, United Kingdom, Ireland, Finland and Spain) using the OECD Analytical database. The exchange rate overvaluation index was extended by applying the rate of change in the average real effective exchange between the 1996-99 and 2000-07 periods to the original 1996-99 index level.

Sala-i-Martin (1997) uses a panel of 134 countries for the period 1960-1992 and tests 62 variables identified previously in the growth literature as significant in at least one growth regression. Using 2 million regressions to test the robustness of the variables to the inclusion of others, the paper identifies 21 which appear to have a stronger relationship with growth, defined as the average growth rate of GDP per capita 1960-1992 i.e. variables with high sign certainty probabilities (i.e. a high proportion of the coefficient estimates fall on the same side of zero).The paper obtains a density of coefficient estimates of the effect on growth for each variable using regressions with different additional variables included. The author defines the strength of the relationship between growth and the explanatory variables in terms of the proportion of the density of the coefficient estimates that is either to the right or left of zero, i.e., for variable 1, if 95% of the density of β 1 estimates lies to the right of zero and only 52% of the density for β 2 estimates for variable 2 lies to the right of zero, then variable 1 is regarded as having a stronger relationship with growth than variable 2. Estimates of the coefficients of the effect of these 21 variables, combined with the original dataset are used to identify the variables and including policy ones that appear to explain the greater part of the growth difference between Mexico and faster growing countries. Mexico is compared to 2 groups, the 10 fastest growing countries over the period and the OECD countries growing faster over the period.

Sala-i-Martin, Doppelhoffer and Miller (2004) use a model-averaging technique to determine which of 67 variables have the strongest relationship with growth in GDP per capita from 1960-1996. Variables are selected on the probability of regressions that contain this variable given the data. In particular, the authors estimate approximately 89 million OLS regressions where the variables are tested with combinations of other explanatory variables. Variables are selected on the basis of the sum of the probabilities given the data of regressions that include that variable (the inclusion probability). This process identifies 21 variables that are "significantly" related to growth i.e. variables with the highest inclusion probabilities and high sign certainty probabilities. Again estimates of the linear marginal effect of each of these 21 variables are used to discover which of these variables appear to be mainly responsible for the difference between Mexico's growth and that of the fastest 10 growing countries in the sample from 1960-1996 and the faster growing OECD countries. Most of these variables are either initial conditions, fixed regional effects or represent factors that are not easily influenced if at all by economic policy.